THE STORYTELLER'S TOOLBOX—VOLUME ONE

THE STORYTELLER'S TOOLBOX—VOLUME ONE

JEFF LYONS

Storygeeks
Press

Rapid Story Development: The Storyteller's Toolbox Volume One

Copyright © 2018 by Jeff Lyons

ISBN: 978-1-7326012-8-4 (e-book)

ISBN: 978-1-7326012-7-7 (print)

Cover art by Jeff Lyons

Interior design by Jeff Lyons

Web: www.jefflyonsbooks.com

First Edition

Printed in the U.S.A

DEDICATION

This is for loyal readers past, present, and future.

Because without you, what's the point?

[SEE NEXT PAGE]

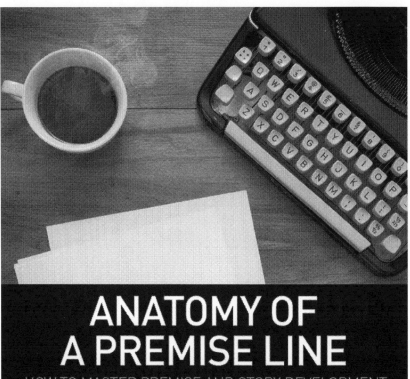

ANATOMY OF
A PREMISE LINE

HOW TO MASTER PREMISE AND STORY DEVELOPMENT
FOR WRITING SUCCESS

JEFF LYONS

ACKNOWLEDGMENTS

The author would like to thank the following individuals for their support, help, encouragement, patience, infinite patience, faith, trust, belief, handouts, generosity, and small petty crimes undertaken to promote the success of this book.

- *Charlene DeLong, Cary Shott,* and *David Allan* —thank you for being trusted beta readers, editors, and telling me the truth.
- Gwen Hayes—for her permissions to reprint her romance genre story beats taken from her book, *Romancing the Beat: Story Structure in Romance Novels.* Contact her and check out her work at: gwenhayes.com/books/nonfiction/

CONTENTS

THE STORYTELLER'S TOOLBOX—
VOLUME ONE

THE STORYTELLER'S
TOOLBOX—VOLUME ONE

PART I

RAPID STORY DEVELOPMENT #1: COMMERCIAL PACE IN FICTION AND CREATIVE NONFICTION

WHAT IS PACE AND WHY SHOULD I CARE?

Pacing refers to the speed of the read and how effectively the text pulls readers into the matter of the book without jolting them with fits and starts or boring them with lengthy, drawn-out exposition. Next to a weak story premise, bad pacing is one of the top-five killers (bad title, weak premise, bad pacing, split stories, episodic writing) of most books. Every book has a pace, just as every book has a voice or a tone. But bad pacing can do more to put off readers than any other single problem.

A reader knows by the end of the first chapter how frenetic or tedious the read is going to be, and if they don't have the patience to hang in there, they will bail before chapter three. If the pace is too slow, it will drag on the reader, sucking their energy, and testing their patience. If the pace is too fast, it will rattle their nerves and distract them with twitchy scenes and shallow writing, often leaving readers annoyed and exasperated.

But, if the pace is right for the story, what I call commercial pace, then the reader is at one with the story and with the writing. They are a partner with the writer, not a tag-along running as fast as they can to keep up, or dragging behind like dead weight.

But, who the heck makes the judgment that a book's writing is too fast, too slow, or just right? Okay, the reader makes the call, but they (with all due respect) are not usually writers themselves; so, what do "they" really know about pacing? And why should you or any writer listen to some third-party casting judgment on your writing? Maybe you want it fast or slow? Slow writing certainly worked for Marcel Proust and James A. Michener. You won't find any black marks next to their names in the Who's Who in Literature warning, "Avoid these writers, they will bore you with slow pacing."

Here's the problem: if you are writing your first book, or maybe the second, you probably do not have the experience to know how to pull off a fast- or slow-paced book without slipping up. Even if you are an experienced novelist, you may never have given this issue any serious consideration. The old maxim "You have to know the rules before you can break them" holds true here. The irony is that there are no rules. No writing police will break down your door and write you a "Poor Pacing Ticket."

There may be no rules; there are, however, best practices. The writing trade has been around a long time, and in that time certain trends, customs, conventions, processes, and procedures have developed that all writers ought to learn and adopt. They do so voluntarily because these best practices have been proven in the field over hundreds of years. And while literary tastes have changed through the ages, best practices have always existed in every literary tradition. And today is no different than one hundred years ago.

So, while there are no hard-and-fast rules, there are the experiences of the many writers who have come before you, and they have set the pace (so to speak) for what is a solid foundation when pacing a book. Do you have to listen to this body of experience? No, of course not. But, if you don't, you risk losing your readers. That's the tradeoff: go it alone and risk losing your target audience or consider the best practices and learn your craft before you write outside the lines.

TAKEAWAY:

- Narrative pace is a tool like any other writing tool.
- Constructing pace is part of being a conscious writer.
- Ignoring pace comes at a high price.

GENRE VS "LITERARY" PACING

Before we get into the specifics of pacing, we should discuss a thorny issue: genre writing versus literary fiction. The consensus view about genre writing (horror, crime, action/adventure, romance, etc.) is that the pacing should be fast, relentless, always building tension and narrative pressure, endlessly raising stakes, and so on. Literary fiction, on the other hand, has the luxury of taking its time, slowing down, savoring the moment, and indulging in narrative tangents, departures, and digressions. In other words, literary fiction can be slow and plodding, but genre fiction should be quick and agile.

While I believe the term "literary fiction" is misleading, and frankly useless (all fiction is literary), the perception I have described is one I appreciate and acknowledge. People are going to make these distinctions between genre and literary fiction regardless of my opinions. Know that everything I will describe in this e-book can apply to any form or style of writing, whether genre or so-called literary writing. The critical factor is not the style of writing, but rather whether or not writers are conscious of what they are doing. The writer must set out to intentionally understand the intended outcome.

THE STRUCTURE OF PACE

Before we examine how pacing works (when it works as intended), or how it fails on the page, it is important to understand that pacing is both an objective and subjective property of writing. It is subjective in that every reader has their own reading experience, and thus how they regard that experience is private and internal. They bring their own biases, assumptions, prejudices, and judgements to the reading process, and therefore make the experience their own. Reading is solitary, singular, and individual.

However, the writer can manipulate this subjective experience using a particular set of tools, techniques, and strategies designed to mold and enhance the reading experience. The writer leverages the structure of pacing to the advantage of the reader and the story being read, thus using objective tools to craft an otherwise personal experience. Narrative pace is therefore intangible at the level of the reader's experience, but very tangible at the level of the page, chapter, and manuscript. In other words, commercial pace in any piece of fiction or creative nonfiction is a physical structure that can be identified and constructed, not unlike story structure itself.

There are four foundation stones of commercial pace:

Pacing Foundation Stones:

- Writing Style
- Chapter Design
- Manuscript Design
- Narrative Drive

Writing Style:

This foundation stone is the one most creative-writing pundits talk about when they try to describe the nuts-and-bolts of narrative pacing. This stone concerns itself almost exclusively with the act of writing, not storytelling or narrative design. Storytelling and writing are two different things that have almost nothing to do with one another (see my book *Anatomy of a Premise Line* [Focal Press] for a more in-depth explanation of this claim). Writing is about language: the rhythm of words, the cadence of syntax and grammar, and the musicality of language itself when used to express thoughts, ideas, and emotions. Writing style is how you individually express all these elements on the page. How you construct a sentence, the words you choose, the flow of the sounds of the words, the linguistic poetry of the written word, etc., can all be used to control the speed of the read and the pace of the reading experience. But, writing style alone is not enough to manage, influence, or establish commercial pace. You need the other three foundation stones.

Chapter Design:

Chapters in a novel, or in a work of creative nonfiction, are constructed using specific narrative tools:

- Story beats
- Scene/scene breaks
- Sequences

A story beat is simply a "bit of business" that establishes a new piece of plotting information; opens a window into a character's emotional or mental process; or introduces a reversal, complication, or reveal that moves the story forward. Beats are the story equivalents of subatomic particles that make up larger forms of matter. These "subatomic" beats are the building blocks of scenes.

A scene is constituted by a collection of beats which occur in the same timeframe, or physical space, and relate to a single point-of-view (POV) character. Generally, a scene break happens whenever you change POV, story time, or story space. Scene breaks are handy tools for controlling pace and the emotional flow of a chapter. Breaks are very often overlooked by writers, rather than seen as the powerful devices they can be for shaping a narrative within a chapter. Scenes (and scene breaks) are the building blocks of sequences.

A scene sequence is three or more scenes that act together to establish significant story milestones that move the story forward. More than a simple beat, and more than a single scene, sequences have more force, direction, and consequence to the movement of a plot than beats or scenes alone, and serve as the real framework for how narrative flows within a chapter.

Chapters are usually made up of at least three scenes (or a scene sequence). Yes, there are examples of writers who don't follow this "rule," such as with the bestselling author James Patterson (we'll see examples of his work later). But, generally speaking, the best approach is to try to construct a chapter so that it has some sense of a beginning, middle, and end (not unlike the story itself). To achieve this flow, the writer needs to have at least three scenes that help build this progression.

These three elements of chapter design (beat, scene/scene break, scene sequence) help the writer systematically piece together a chapter that has forward momentum, narrative drive, and structural integrity. The key to pacing at this level is developing a sense of mystery or suspense whenever you exit a scene, scene sequence, or chapter. The final chapter in this e-book, "Narrative Drive," will go into more detail about how to accomplish this in practice.

Manuscript Design:

Beyond the issues of book parts, sections, etc. (as defined by *The Chicago Manual of Style*) manuscripts have a natural structure that powerfully contributes to the creation of commercial pace.

This structure occurs at the page level, chapter level, and the overall level of the manuscript. In a very real way, this last foundation stone holds within it the other three stones (*writing style, chapter design, narrative drive*). Here we have a kind of summation of scene, page, and chapter that makes accessible the five essential elements required to create a satisfying commercial pace for any manuscript.

The Five Essential Elements of Manuscript Design:

- Number of words per page
- Number of pages per chapter
- Overall number of chapters
- Overall manuscript word count
- Overall manuscript page count

At the manuscript level, these five elements are always present and are literally physical structures in the writing that contribute to overall pacing in a book. As you can see from each bullet, their meanings are self-explanatory. We will see how they are used in the next couple of chapters.

Narrative Drive:

Working along with the other three foundation stones is this thing called narrative drive. This is such an important piece of commercial pace that I have devoted the entire last chapter to this topic. Narrative drive is infused throughout scenes, chapters, and the manuscript as a whole. It is the impulse to keep reading, and it is something that you as the writer have full control over as you design your narrative. But, before you jump to the last chapter, take the time to learn about the other foundation stones so that you have a deeper appreciation for pacing once you get to narrative drive.

Each foundation stone works with all the other stones to create a synergy. The term synergy derives from the Greek words "synergia" (συνεργία) and "synergos" (συνεργός), meaning "working together." When two or more things are in synergy, they work together to produce something that would otherwise be unachievable working alone. Alone, they are each simply pieces of the structure of a book. But, when they are working together they produce something neither of them could create alone: commercial pace.

When writing style, chapter design, manuscript design, and narrative drive are working together, when everything is in balance, the following qualities are produced:

- The reader is engaged in a way that does not distract or disrupt the reading experience.
- The reader becomes oblivious to the fact that they are reading; "the read" just happens.
- Plot, character development, and story structure drive the story forward with no help from writing tricks or linguistic workarounds.

So, the question now becomes, how do you balance the stones? How do you leverage this tangible structure commercial pace for the greatest possible result for the reader? The easiest way to learn how to structure good pacing is to examine what pacing looks like when it is working, and conversely what it looks like when it is not working.

WHERE PACING GOES RIGHT: COMMERCIAL PACE

There are simple steps you can take to assure that your book is properly paced for the story you want to tell. Before I show you how pacing can go wrong, and the effects this can have on a narrative, let's first look at how pacing can go right.

The concept of "commercial pace" is not a publishing industry *term d'art*, but rather a term I coined to describe books that tightly hold a reader's interest, engage their imagination, keep them entertained, and do all of these things regardless of the length of the book. Books I've read that do all of these things seamlessly are few and far between. Even in the world of commercial fiction, solid commercial pace is uncommon. Even practiced novelists have challenges with pacing their work, but new and inexperienced writers are more than challenged, pacing problems plague them. Getting the right speed for the read is part science, part art, and part having a great editor. It also means knowing the structure of pace and how to use all the pieces as a conscious writer.

Profile of a Well-Paced Book

A well-paced book has specific properties that can be readily identified. These properties don't have to be exact, but they represent solid guidelines any writer can follow. These properties are made up of the five manuscript-level components of commercial pace (listed earlier) in a specific configuration that can be duplicated in any work of fiction or creative nonfiction.

There are some assumptions we can make, however, before we define our components of commercial pace. These assumptions are not random, or subjective, they are taken from the current traditional, subsidy, and self-publishing industries' best practices, and when used along with the five components they help us define and refine our approach to pacing.

Three Assumptions:

- Chapter Page Count: Optimal chapter lengths are between 8–15 pages (fiction), and 15–25 pages (nonfiction).
- Words Per Printed Page: Average number of words on a printed page is 250 words.
- Overall Page Count: Maximum manuscript page count is approximately 400 pages.

The overall min-max page count is based on the fact that many publishers are reluctant to publish books over 400 pages due to the costs of shipping and printing a book of that size. Bookstores likewise are reluctant to carry large books because shelf space is a premium. It is rare for them to take on a large-sized book by a first-time or unproven writer, as the expenses involved are often unrecouped. Electronic books can have more latitude than printed books, as e-reading devices can play with innovative book applications, formats, and physical presentation in a way print books cannot.

The average number of words on a page is a long-standing convention used to estimate page size in a printed book. Different print formats (paperback, trade paperback, or custom sizes) will vary in word count per page, especially if non-standard fonts and styles are used, but 250 words are the general rule of thumb. Publishers will very often condense text on the page by messing around with line spacing and line heights to cut down on page count (i.e., print costs). Despite all these pitfalls, writers should use the 250-word standard.

Having chapter lengths between 8 and 15 pages is a generalized average based on contemporary standards in fiction. Again, some authors do more, many authors do less, but the average tends to fall within this range. This also seems to be a popular comfort zone for readers. If you research various reader blog sites on the Internet that discuss these issues, you will find these page ranges to be commonly mentioned.

TAKEAWAY:

- Every book has a natural pace for the story being told.
- Mixing pace (fast/slow) can work, but be careful.

- Pace can make or break your book's readability.

So, based on the above three assumptions, and combined with the five components of commercial pace, the optimal, well-paced book will have the following profile:

- Overall word count: 75,000–100,000 words
- Overall page count: 300–400 pages
- Average number of pages per chapter: fiction 8–15 pages, nonfiction 15–25 pages
- Overall number of chapters (fiction):

Page Count	@15pgs/ Chpt	@25pgs/ Chpt
300	37.5	20
400	50	27

- Overall number of chapters (nonfiction):

Page Count	@15pgs/ Chpt	@25pgs/ Chpt
300	20	12
400	27	16

Many books by self-published authors fall within this general page range of 300 to 400 pages, so these guidelines are reasonably practical. However, you are not stuck in this range.

You can do less or more, but these are the guidelines to use to orient yourself. If you can come close to keeping the five components in proportion (as described earlier) in whatever page and word counts you end up with, then you will at least have a fighting chance to have a well-paced book. This also does not mean you can't mix it up (some short chapters, some long). Artistic license gives you full reign to do what you want, but if you keep these guidelines in mind, you will at least have some control over your pacing at a structural level, regardless of how you play with the individual components.

Now that we have a profile of a book that is well paced let's look at how can this go wrong in actual execution. Fortunately, there are only two basic scenarios that will come into play: books paced too slowly, and books paced too quickly.

WHERE PACING GOES WRONG: SLOW PACING

How can a book's pace be too slow? What does "too slow" even mean? Slow in relation to what? After all, don't people read books for the pleasure of reading? Don't they expect lots of words, long passages of description, super-detailed character portraits, and voluminous exposition of scenery and settings? Some readers do expect these things. Some read for the sheer joy of the written word. Story, plot, and commercial appeal are not issues that concern them. If they wanted to read something easy on the brain, they'd pick up a graphic novel, not *Swann's Way* by Marcel Proust.

Granted, "slow" is a subjective and relative term in this context. Perhaps it will help to talk, not in terms of some ill defined concept of speed, but rather concerning a reader's experience. When you read a book and find yourself reading pages of description, and then you suddenly find yourself wondering about what you'll have for dinner, the story has lost you as a reader. When you start skipping paragraphs or pages because you want to get to the next bit of action or see where the last scene ends up, the story has lost you as a reader. When you slog through pages of exposition and then come to some sense of completion, but find yourself forgetting what happened before the exposition started, then the story has lost you as a reader.

These are all examples of how the reader's experience can be derailed by poor pacing. Slow pacing also has specific effects on the narrative itself:

- It distances the reader from the material by stopping the forward momentum of the plot; e.g., the story stops for a five-page description of the roses outside the window.
- It is a form of authorial intrusion because it draws the reader's attention away from the story and to the author's writing; e.g., "See me, see how great I am at describing a rose bush! Aren't I a great writer?"
- It adds unnecessary pages to the book, thus raising the costs of printing and shipping for the author, or a book distributor.
- It discourages a reader from continuing to read and opens the door for them to bail and go watch TV.

An example from literature will help to illustrate some of these points, especially the point about there not being any hard-and-fast rules. One of my favorite authors is James A. Michener, and he is one of the worst violators of the slow-pacing problem. This is an author with a Pulitzer Prize, millions of fans, and legendary status as a prized American author. And he wrote some of the worst-paced books ever published. Why do people read his books and yet seem to ignore his pacing problems? Because, as a great storyteller and a great writer, he can pull it off. When you have his kind of talent, you can follow your own rules and people will still love you. Such was and continues to be, the case with Michener's books. Michener knew what he was doing and was able to compensate for structural and story weaknesses with great writing. As I remarked earlier in this book, sheer talented writing has saved many a bad or poorly paced story.

As an example, our test case will be Michener's *Centennial*. Depending on which edition you read, this book is between 900 and 1038 pages; not exactly light reading. At the start of the book, the first chapter, "The Commission," sets up the story of a fictional writer being hired to write the history of the region and the town of Centennial, Colorado. The next two chapters, "The Land" and "The Inhabitants," totalling roughly 91 pages, describe the formation of the Earth, especially the Rocky Mountains and the land directly around Centennial. A series of mini-stories follow, depicting the region's animals that lived over the aeons in what would become Centennial, from the dinosaur Diplodocus to the arrival of man.

The rest of the book deals with human beings (a great many different human beings), their personal stories, and the rise of the American West. But it's that span of 91 pages that takes readers through the prehistory of the Earth, and life itself, that sends many readers running screaming down the hall. It's this kind of writing that gives Michener the reputation for writing books that start with the Big Bang and then, a thousand pages later, comes to some present-day story. This may be a gross exaggeration, of course, but all such exaggerations start with some grain of truth, e.g., *Centennial*.

Michener's writing style is the epitome of slow pacing. A lesser writer might have started the story a little closer to the end, say a few million years after the primordial ooze formed. In the case of *Centennial*, readers have to slog through almost 100 pages of geology and paleontology before getting to a human story! This may be great stuff for Michener fans, but for the average reader, this slog would send them reaching for a good mystery novel.

The argument against what I'm saying, of course, is that Michener has millions of books in print. Clearly, he must know something I don't know about what works and doesn't work in a novel. I won't wrestle with that one, other than to say that the success of *Centennial*, including being picked up for a 12-episode TV miniseries, was due to the talent of the writer and the magic of his writing, not the mistakes he made in some of his books. Michener, like many great writers, pulled it off despite himself. Would you be so lucky? This is the real question you need to be asking.

If you are writing your first, second, or even your third book, do you have the raw talent to go it alone and buck best practices? The proof will be in the publishing. My advice is to err on the side of caution and follow these basic guidelines. When you start feeling your stride as a writer, perhaps experiment and start your books at the beginning of the Universe. But, until that time, the next chapter will tell you how you avoid the pitfalls of slow pacing in your self-published book.

HOW TO SPEED UP SLOW PACING

In the words of Sir Arthur Quiller-Couch, "Murder your darlings." He was referring, of course, to any writer's "impulse to perpetrate a piece of exceptionally fine writing." Killing your darlings is one of the hardest things a writer has to do, but when the darlings get in the way, they have to be removed—we're talking cutting and editing here, for the squeamish among you.

As I described earlier in this e-book, scenes make up sequences, sequences make up chapters, and chapters make up books. Beyond the scene and chapter levels, there are additional structural pacing techniques that the writer should consider at the scene and chapter levels, besides the *essential five components* mentioned earlier.

When it comes to scene, sequence, and chapter design the author should ask the following questions per scene/sequence:

- *Does the exposition in question move the plot forward?*

Let's say your protagonist is about to walk into the haunted house and encounter the killer poltergeist, and you decide to tell the reader about the rich lineage of the rosebushes lining the staircase to the front door. These bushes go back hundreds of years to the original seed pods used by Marie Antoinette. This exposition will take 15 pages, but the history is so rich and wonderful, and you have so many adverbs and adjectives ready at your fingertips. Has the real story stopped? The plot was moving forward when your protagonist walks up the front steps to the door. Did the plot stop dead in its tracks with the roses? The answer is—yes. Examine every choice to break into expository writing. How does it help the previous action? How does it help the current action? Does it enhance the next story beat, or does it derail the scene's momentum? Ask these fundamental questions (and related questions), and then tell yourself the truth. If the action stops, kill your darlings.

- *Is the scene about a person?*

Stories are about people, human beings having a set of experiences leading to emotional change. Every scene in a story must support this principle. Every scene needs to have a person at its core, not a mountain range, not a chocolate cake, not a sport or a purely abstract idea, but a person. If the scene is not about a person, then it can probably be deleted. It's possible, for reasons of pure exposition, that it might work to have a scene focus on an inanimate object (e.g., as setup for another scene), but generally this is not a good idea. This is your call as the writer, as you know your story's requirements, but try to keep a human focus even at the scene level.

- *If dialogue is present in the scene, is it relevant?*

Expository prose is not the only way to slow down a scene. Just as you could deliver the history of rosebushes in tedious prose, your protagonist could recite in dialogue a similar 15-page account of the roses to the cop who arrests her for breaking into the haunted house. It's possible a long, crazy speech about roses could be a character window, a means to show how off-center the heroine has become, but this effect could probably be accomplished in a few paragraphs, rather than 15 pages. The talking points don't add to the plot, they don't set up new action, nor do they enhance the current action. Conversation along these lines would be nothing more than pointless exposition in the form of dialogue.

In the same way that there are questions you can ask at the scene level to avoid or fix pacing problems, there are also some questions you can ask yourself at the chapter level to facilitate better pacing.

- *At the chapter level, are chapter lengths consistent with the principles of commercial pace?*

Chapter length should fall within a range of page that allows for proper character development and plot development (fiction: 8–15 pages, nonfiction: 15–25 pages). There are exceptions to this guideline, but for new and inexperienced writers it is easy to lose track of chapter lengths and end up with very long chapters, or with a mix of short and long chapters. Even if chapters end up on the long side, the writer should try to keep them roughly uniform throughout the book. Consistently paced chapters help to maintain a uniform read, even if scenes stray and go off on expository tangents.

- *Are chapter intros and extros effectively transitioning the reader into the chapter and out of the chapter?*

How you get into the substance of a chapter (intro) is critical for conveying a sense of setting the tone of the chapter's pace. The chapter intro is the "bit of business" (story beat) that introduces the chapter's POV character, and it usually happens in the first paragraph (or second, at the latest). It needs to be something clever, interesting, and visual if possible. This is how you get the reader into the chapter, so make it attention-grabbing. Likewise, how you leave the chapter is essential for jumpstarting the reader into the next chapter.

The chapter extro is how the chapter ends and sets up the transition to the next chapter. Is the POV character left, in the end, with a question? Do they learn something new? Do they survive the attack, and if so, do they have a plan for what to do next? Any action that concludes a chapter or scene should demonstrate the emotional and physical disposition of the POV character at the end of the chapter or scene.

- *Does the chapter have a clear sense of a beginning, middle, and end?*

Pacing and flow feel complete and satisfying when the structure of the chapter mirrors the flow of the manuscript as a whole. That is: if the story has a beginning, middle, and end—then so should each chapter. There is a natural sense of completion that comes from starting, engaging, and ending something. That sense is lost when chapters are only one or two short scenes in length. These snippets might be interesting beats in and of themselves, but they lack the satisfaction that comes from a well-paced chapter. Popular fiction, especially genre fiction, is notorious for short chapters of one or two scenes (see our example soon with James Patterson's book).

TAKEAWAY:

- Pace doesn't "just happen," you control it as the writer.
- Chapter design is the royal road to perfect pacing.
- Never leave a chapter without giving the reader a reason to turn the page.

The writers who rely on this technique of writing are highly influenced (in my opinion) by film and television scriptwriting, where the focus is on the scene or scene sequence. This influence is positive in many ways, but for prose writers, the screenwriting approach to prose fiction/nonfiction is a dangerous influence when they have yet to master one or both forms of writing. Only after a writer has genuinely mastered screenwriting can they effectively write short scenes capable of packing in enough story gold to support a chapter-length of two to four pages.

Interestingly, and to his credit, James Patterson has said that short chapters are his writing style, and it would be disastrous if everyone wrote the way he did. (One more reason for loving James Patterson.)

WHERE PACING GOES WRONG: FAST PACING

The other side of the pacing coin appears when the pace is too fast. Once again, "fast" is a matter of subjective experience. Who's to say what fast is? As with slow pacing, judging excessive pace means considering the reader's experience. If as a reader you find yourself starting a chapter and then suddenly you are segued to the next in the blink of an eye, then the story has left you in the dust. If you find yourself constantly wondering who the characters are, if you never see them beneath the surface, then the story has sped past you. If you finish the book feeling like you have been on a wild ride, only to look back and wonder, "What was all the fuss about?" then the story was moved so quickly as to be a blur.

These experiences all describe a typical reader's reactions to a pace that moves too fast at the expense of the narrative. Whereas slow pacing implies an overabundance of words, fast pace is usually recognizable by concise, staccato chapters, or by chapters composed of only one scene, or by an abbreviated overall word count that inhibits the writer's ability to achieve any depth. The specific effects this all has on the narrative includes the following:

- A pace that continually yanks the reader in and out of the action scenes, making it hard for them to focus and fully engage.
- A pace that makes it impossible for the writer to achieve any real depth in plotting or character development.
- A pace that makes it difficult to produce compelling, dramatic momentum through the middle of the story.
- A pace that ultimately distances the reader from the material because it never lets them fully into the character's inner life, instead of trying to hook the reader with one action beat after another.

An example from literature will illustrate the point. James Patterson is one of the most successful suspense writers in the history of the genre. He was one of the first mainstream genre authors with a traditional publishing deal to sell over a million e-books. He has over fifty *New York Times* bestselling titles. Patterson is famous for his Alex Cross novels and multiple other series, including his popular "Women's Murder Club" mystery series. By any measure he is a wildly successful author; we should all be so lucky. But, like Michener, he is a wild success despite himself. Patterson is one of the worst violators of the "speed laws" of fast pacing.

Take, for example, his *1st to Die: A Women's Murder Club Mystery*. This is one of the few titles that Patterson actually wrote solo; he is famous (or infamous, depending on who you talk to) for having numerous writing partners who pen most of his works as "co-writers," a practice for which he is widely criticized. In a "10 Questions" interview in the July 5, 2010, issue of *Time Magazine*, Patterson was asked, "What do you say to critics like author Stephen King who say you're not a great prose stylist?" Patterson responded, "I am not a great prose stylist. I'm a storyteller. There are thousands of people who don't like what I do. Fortunately, there are millions who do." (Despite my own criticisms of Patterson, I highly respect him as an authorpreneur and as an advocate for the writing vocation.)

1st to Die is a wonderful example of pace run amuck, and a textbook example of a masterful writer who saves the day anyway. Here is the pacing profile for *1st to Die*:

- 462 pages in length.
- 127 chapters.
- the approximate overall word count for the novel is 116,000 words.
- and the average chapter length is 3.6 pages.

Based on our previous discussion of commercial pace and the profile of a well-paced book, it should be clear that this is not a well-paced book. It would be instructive here to analyze *1st to*

Die to see how it could be brought into line and "fixed," because these attributes are typical of many genre (horror, mystery, romance, thriller, etc.) novels and memoirs by self-published authors. But, that examination will have to wait for a couple of chapters. First, we should look look at a useful approach for slowing down a too-fast-paced book.

HOW TO SLOW DOWN FAST PACING

Whereas slow pacing is about condensing, deleting, and editing out extraneous material, fast pacing requires the opposite approach. The writer needs to step back and examine each scene and chapter to decide what needs expansion, what needs deepening in the narrative, and the efficiency of overall scene and chapter organization.

Can short chapters be combined to give a "super-short" chapter more depth?

Chapters that are made up of only one or two scenes are inadequate to engage readers fully. Often when writers break up chapters into such short scenes, they follow each "chapter" with a scene that could easily be included in the previous "chapter." You should group enough scenes together to give each chapter at least three scenes. (The reason for three will be explained a bit later; it is not a random number picked out of the air.)

For example, if your protagonist has broken into the haunted house, and the opening scene of the chapter shows her cracking open a safe where some clue is hidden (known only to her), she could find something unexpected in the safe that sends her into a flashback that reveals a key backstory factoid, which in turn helps the reader appreciate the next scene or chapter, thus moving the story forward. This is an example of adding a backstory exposition to the text to deepen the plot and the character.

CAN SHORT CHAPTERS BE EXPANDED WITHOUT COMBINING THEM WITH OTHER CHAPTERS?

Short chapters can also simply be expanded independently of the chapters around them. Subtext, backstory, and character development can all help to build out and deepen a chapter.

There are some basic questions that the author can ask him or herself, at the chapter level, that can help shed light on missed opportunities to expand the text constructively:

- Is there a subtext that could prompt backstory exposition, helping readers to understand the context of the scene fully?
- Does the point of view (POV) character in the scene exhibit behaviors that have been fully explained by previous exposition or backstory?
- Do supporting characters in the scene make dramatic sense; meaning, does their relationship to the POV

character go beyond the simple, surface actions occurring on the page?

- Does the reader know everything they need to know to understand fully what is motivating the scene's POV character and the full context of the action?
- Does the POV character's internal dialogue/motivations provide windows into their character and relevant backstory?
- Is the scene necessary? Does it move the main plot forward, or does it add extraneous information that if deleted would not be missed?

CAN A BASIC RESTRUCTURING OF CHAPTERS, BOOK PARTS (IF APPLICABLE), AND CHAPTER LENGTHS MAKE A DIFFERENCE?

This is the basic approach suggested above in the discussion for proper pacing and the optimal pacing profile. Could basic changes to the pacing structure be enough to fix the problem of speed? Let's look at that sample diagnostic of James Patterson's novel from the previous chapter and see how the approach we've covered might be a partial solution in this test case.

A PACING DIAGNOSTIC

Let's look at James Patterson's *1st to Die* as our test case for this diagnostic. What would a good developmental editor say to a first-time writer with the pacing profile numbers as this novel? They would say that the short chapter lengths are a huge problem, that three or four pages per chapter are barely enough to introduce a scene. This extreme brevity is why this author needs nearly 130 chapters to tell the story. The short chapter lengths and the huge number of chapters keep the reader jumping in and out of chapters at a frantic pace. Yes, they will have a page-turner on their hands (literally), but many readers, accustomed to turning pages in pleasurable anticipation of what's next will find turning pages so rapidly, to keep up, downright annoying. They might prefer to settle in and take more than ninety seconds to read a whole chapter. The author's decision to use super-short chapters, dictating the need for a large number of overall chapters, results in a pace that will frazzle most readers who are not diehard fans of the author.

If the overall word count is to remain the same, then the author should restructure the work using the following guidelines:

- The current pacing profile for this work stands as follows:

Overall Word Count	Overall Page Count	Avg Pgs/ Chpt	Total # of Chpts
116K	464	3.6	129

- Re-examine each chapter to see if combining chapters will help cut down on the overall number of chapters.
- If combining chapters is not possible, then re-examine chapters composed of only one scene and find a way to add at least two more scenes to give the chapter a sense of some beginning, middle, and end. This may not always be possible, but one-scene chapters are not good writing style and do not support building a narrative.
- Shoot for chapters of at least eight pages in length, which would more than double the current average length (note: eight pages falls at the low end of the recommended page range for a novel, thus keeping with the author's desire for having shorter, not longer, chapters).

At an overall word count of 116,000 words, the book will come in at approximately 464 pages when printed. If you use eight pages per chapter as a guide, that count will yield 58 chapters overall.

- The final pacing profile for this work would then be:

Overall Word Count	Overall Page Count	Avg Pgs/ Chpt	Total # of Chpts
116K	464	8	58

Based on this new profile, the book will have a more steady read, be less jolting and disruptive to the reader, and afford the writer more opportunities to deepen the narrative.

The above analysis of Patterson's *1st to Die* might seem presumptuous to many, considering the book's huge success. But, once again I assert: A poorly paced narrative can be pulled from the fire by snappy writing and a loyal fan base. Successful sales alone don't mean that execution wasn't without its flaws, or that there wasn't a problem with craft. And believe it or not, real creative accomplishment sometimes isn't about the money: Art and craft matter, and sometimes they can be the only incentives a writer needs.

NARRATIVE DRIVE

66 NARRATIVE DRIVE *is the quality any story possesses that excites a reader to continue reading."*

Many writing gurus and creative writing teachers talk about the importance of keeping the story moving forward. They all teach that any story should build, have tension, have momentum, directionality, energy, and so on. And many give ideas on how to accomplish these things. But, few if any make the critical connection between narrative drive and narrative pace, in the context that I have discussed pace throughout this e-book.

For many, I think, drive and pace are almost interchangeable, and I can understand how this mistaken idea might be made. In a very surface way, the two terms (drive and pace) suggest some of the same functions. When you imagine them both, you think of movement, and you feel forward motion—if not literally, then certainly in some implied way. Drive and pace, however, are two different things, and one of them is subordinate to the other.

The bottom line for the reader is that they are either engaged by a story enough to want to turn the page or they are not. It's that straightforward. Readers will often give the writer several opportunities to engage them, but if the story should slip into torpor or inertia, the writer had better kick things into gear because the reader will not wait forever.

If the story doesn't "wake up" and start doing all the things it's supposed to be doing (raising stakes, building tension, having energy, etc.) then the reader will walk away and probably never come back. Narrative drive, along with the earlier structural and language-based pacing techniques discussed earlier in this e-book (writing style, chapter design, manuscript design) is a powerful pacing tool that when wielded skillfully by the writer can assure reader engagement—thus narrative drive is at the service of and subordinate to the function of commercial pace.

This is an essential relationship every writer needs to understand, because if you separate narrative drive and pace and treat them as disconnected things, the chances they will be at odds and potentially cancel one another out increases, and rather than helping your development effort you more likely will end up hampering it.

Almost everyone reduces narrative drive down to the "simple" task of creating a sense of mystery, suspense, or dramatic irony. The suggestion is that if you create a question worth of answering or slip a bomb under someone's chair or get ironic, then you are home safe—instant narrative drive. I wish it were that easy.

Still, others give copious examples of scenes in movies and novels that put readers on the edge of their seats, or raise expectations, or threaten increased danger, but provide little direction how to do these things yourself, as if to say, "Just do what they did."

None of them is wrong, I simply don't think they go far enough to help writers understand how narrative drive works and what writers can do as writers to execute it on the page in a deliberate way. So, let's start to unpack this problem and demystify the nuts and bolts of narrative drive.

HOW NARRATIVE DRIVE WORKS

In keeping with the underlying theme of all the e-books in the "Rapid Story Development" series, the idea of the conscious writer applies here. Rather than repeat what others say about narrative drive, the objective now is to go deeper into the subject so that you can make informed creative choices about how you want to build and deliver this experience in any story, not merely parrot one or another narrative technique or example.

Narrative drive is primal in that it responds to and excites four primary emotions in readers (it should be noted that these can also be mental states):

- Curiosity

- Anxiety
- Apprehension
- Anticipation

Every human being feels these emotions, so they are familiar to everyone. Some of them are pleasant, and some of them are unpleasant. But as long as we can feel them on our terms, i.e., in a two-hour movie we can leave, or reading a book we can close, we will enjoy feeling all of these emotions, knowing there will be no real-world consequences to the feeling. We call that being entertained.

Consuming any piece of narrative fiction, regardless of the form, will bring up many more emotions than these four, but these listed above are the ones primarily responsible for generating narrative drive.

They can be understood as follows:

- *Curiosity*: a strong desire to know or learn something.
- *Anticipation*: generalized expectation, a known or predictable result, not fear or anxiety based, prepared for outcomes, eagerness to know.
- *Apprehension*: dread, an unknown result, fear and anxiety based, unprepared for outcomes, generalized uncertainty.
- *Anxiety*: fear of the unknown, an unspecified fear.

When you create any of these emotions in your characters, you will generate narrative drive. These are the brass rings you want to reach for when you design story beats, individual scenes, scene sequences, and chapter exists (see chapter two, "The Structure of Pace" for term definitions).

HOW TO CREATE NARRATIVE DRIVE

Mystery and suspense don't create these four emotions; they are simply convenient containers that carry the feelings and represent literary techniques that naturally lend themselves to one or more of these four emotions. In other words, telling a writer to create a sense of mystery or suspense in a scene or chapter exit is not enough to properly develop a sense of narrative drive. The writer needs to be conscious about what he or she is doing, i.e., know what they are writing and why they are writing it (part of being a conscious writer).

If they are going for a sense of apprehension, then suspense is a good catchall container to frame out how to write the scene so that it creates anxiety and apprehension. If you are going for curiosity and a "let's see what happens next" feeling, then you will want to create mystery and expectation. It is not the mystery or suspense that creates the narrative drive; it is the emotion(s) associated with mystery or suspense that propel the story forward. This is so critically important to understand because blindly picking a mysterious or suspenseful scenario, without knowing if it is the best choice for the point-of-view (POV) character in the scene or chapter, can lead to misfires and clumsy setups and payoffs.

MYSTERY VS SUSPENSE

At this point, it would be beneficial to establish a clear foundation for using these important terms, as they are often confused and misused by writers. Mystery and suspense are, in fact, different emotional and mental dramatic processes.

Mystery

Mystery is primarily a mental process of calculation, analysis, information filtering, information processing, etc. There are emotions involved, but they are not intense or deep or moving the way they are in suspense. From an emotional perspective, mystery is about curiosity, expectation, surprise, and anticipation (and all their associated feelings; see earlier definitions).

When the term mystery is used, in a dramatic context, it almost always refers to the central mystery, i.e., the mystery that spans the course of an entire story. There are, of course, little mysteries along the way in any story; questions that must be answered, or puzzles that must be solved. But, generally speaking, when someone says they are writing a mystery, they mean they are creating an overarching question that can only be answered across the entirety of a story.

Any smaller mysteries that might pop up along the way are usually breadcrumbs that lead to clues to help solve the central mystery, and gathering these crumbs provides a level of emotional satisfaction for the reader as they get incrementally closer to the final solution. The key to appreciating mystery lies in understanding that it rests on the principle of withholding from the reader and protagonist. The writer intentionally holds back information and only trickles it out slowly over the course of the story as the protagonist, or other characters, become deserving of it.

It is interesting to note that Alfred Hitchcock, the famous film director of *Psycho, The Birds,* and *Rear Window* (among others) disliked mysteries and favored suspense stories, precisely because mysteries were not emotional enough for him. For emotion, Hitchcock's goto form was suspense.

Suspense:

Suspense is primarily an emotional, dramatic process generating anxiety, fear, apprehension, insecurity, and uncertainty. There are mental processes that take place too, but whatever problem solving or analysis might be involved, they are secondary to the emotional turmoil of feeling suspended in a limbo of emotional anxiety and mental not-knowing.

When the term suspense is used in a dramatic context, it too refers to an emotional state that spans the entire story, not only segments or specific scenes. The emotional suspension of unease and tension is relentless and builds as the story develops. Whereas mystery is based on withholding information from the reader and protagonist, suspense is based on selective withholding. The one lacking in this situation is the protagonist, and the one "in the know" is the reader.

The classic scenario demonstrating this distinction is the one where two people sit in a restaurant eating dinner. Suddenly, a bomb goes off under the table, and they are killed. The reader is as surprised as the victims. The reader didn't know anything about the bomb, nor did the victims. This is a mystery: a whodunit.

Contrast this to the next scenario. The same table at the restaurant, but the reader is privy to the killer placing the bomb under the table five minutes before the victims arrive. The victims arrive and begin their leisurely dinner. The clock is ticking. The reader knows all; the victims are clueless. This is suspense.

So, which is better to use: mystery or suspense? Neither one is better, but the situation you are creating at the scene or chapter level in your story will often dictate which of the two is more appropriate. You have to use your creative and technical judgement to make a decision. The choice you make, however, should not be careless on your part.

Most story experts will not talk about the danger in randomly choosing your method of developing narrative drive (mystery vs suspense); they will merely tell you those are your choices, so pick one. Rather than gamble, I suggest you decide what you want and then make an informed creative choice. Because the real dramatic gold isn't the choice of mystery or suspense; the real treasures are the emotions under the surface of those two frameworks. Know what you're going for emotionally under the surface, then make your choice: mystery or suspense.

ANOTHER WAY INTO NARRATIVE DRIVE

I have suggested that achieving narrative drive means generating an impulse on the part of the reader to move forward with the story, i.e., turn the page. This impulse is not some generic thing but created by the writer leveraging four specific emotions to create specific impulses leading to a sense of mystery or suspense.

There is another way into narrative drive; however, that also gets you to the same result without knowing upfront which emotional brass rings you want. It is not a better way; it's a different one. It is the relationship the reader has with the POV character in a scene or chapter vis-a-vis point of view itself.

In any scene or chapter, there is usually one POV character. They may be the central hero or heroine, but not necessarily. Some writers like to mix up POV characters within scenes or chapters, but this is usually a bad idea, as it splits the dramatic focus of the scene, but also the focus of the reader. So, I'm going to adopt the best practice here of suggesting a single POV character per scene or chapter.

The reader and POV character share an exceptional relationship in relation to any story's action. They can share the same POV, the reader can have a superior POV, or the reader can have an inferior POV. If the reader has a superior POV, then they know more about what is going on in the scene than the character. If the reader has an inferior POV, then the character knows more about what is happening than the reader. If they share an equal POV then, obviously, they both have an equal view of the action. Each these positions: equal, superior, inferior generates either a sense of mystery or suspense.

EQUAL POSITION:

The POV character and the reader share the same level of knowledge and understanding about what is happening, why it's happening, and how it's happening. Whatever the POV character learns, the reader learns at the same time. Whatever new awareness is gained by the POV character that propels the story forward, the reader becomes aware of at the same time.

Most importantly, the reader and POV character are equally in the dark about what is going to happen next, and there is either anxiety or fear generated about any future action. Whenever the reader encounters this form of suspense, they are as equally uncertain, anxious and curious as the POV character. The impulse is to relieve the anxiety, and the only way to do that is to keep reading, i.e., find out what the future holds. The impulse (narrative drive) that emerges from this position is the *suspense* that comes from apprehension (fear or anxiety of the future). The prevailing emotional and mental state is uncertainty. Emotional uncertainty about how good or bad the future might feel, and mental uncertainty because outcomes are ambiguous.

SUPERIOR POSITION:

The reader has a superior level of knowledge and understanding about what is happening, why it's happening, or how it's happening than the POV character. They might initially feel good about being ahead of the plot curve, in relation to the POV character, but what they don't know is how that character is going to react when he or she knows what the reader knows. This creates an impulse of suspense, the strong sense that something will happen but what that thing is remains shrouded and hidden. It might be unknown for now, but it is coming.

If for some reason that POV character never gets there and is unable to catch up with the reader, then there will be a sense of dread on the part of the reader, "Oh my, what will happen to them if they fail to learn what I know?" This is still part of the suspense framework. The prevailing emotional state is in this situation is anxiety, and the mental state is one of apprehension.

INFERIOR POSITION:

The reader has a lesser or lower level of awareness and understanding about what is happening, why it's happening, or how it's happening than the POV character. The reader is always playing catchup, trying to piece together bits of information to see the whole picture of the story's action.

Most importantly, the reader is trying to solve the question of what is next, not from a position of dread or anxiety, but from a position of expectancy , "I know there is more, and I'll find it." They have some information, maybe a lot of information, but not as much as the POV character. The impulse that emerges from this relationship is the mystery of curiosity (a strong desire to know or learn something). The prevailing emotion state is anticipation, while the mental state is analytical. Even if the reader is spinning mental wheels to catch up, and getting nowhere, they are still calculating and analyzing, trying to connect story dots and make inferences from story events to find equal ground with the POV character.

DRAMATIC IRONY

Dramatic irony is almost a special case of narrative drive because so many story experts mention it in any analysis of drive. For many, dramatic irony is seen as its own animal because the primary emotional response to it by characters who experience it is dread. Dread is often considered a separate road into narrative drive, along with mystery and suspense. I believe this is an erroneous consideration. For me, dramatic irony is simply another form of suspense and should not be separated as its own category.

Dramatic irony is defined, in the classic sense, as a situation where the full meaning and implication of one character's words or actions are clear to the reader but unclear or unknown to another character. Here are a couple of examples of dramatic irony from the worlds of literature and film:

Example: *A Doll's House* (play by Henrik Ibsen)

"To be able to be free from care, quite free from care; to be able to play and romp with the children; to be able to keep the house beautifully and have everything just as Torvald likes it!"

Nora, one of the main characters, is brightly looking forward to a time when she would be free of her debts to another character in the play. However, her dialogue becomes dramatic irony when the audience knows that her sense of freedom is actually servitude, which she comes to realize only in the end.

Example: *Night of the Living Dead* (by John Russo, George Romero, Living Dead Media, 1968)

A group of people fight zombies in a country house and at the end of the movie the sole human survivor, Ben, emerges from the basement to live another day. But, when the authorities are moving through the community, "cleaning up" the zombie threat, they see Ben in a window of the house and shoot him, thinking he is undead. The audience is the only one who knows the meaning of this killing—the cops never know the truth of what they have done.

These two different examples of dramatic irony (one shown in dialogue and the other shown in page action) set up a superior position vis-a-vis the reader and the POV character in the story. The reader knows more and as a result develops a sense of dread for the POV character and experiences anxiety from the suspense of waiting for the final reveal, "Oh my, what will become of them when they learn the truth?" Thus, dramatic irony is not a separate category of narrative drive, but merely another form of suspense delivered through a popular and well-known literary device.

So to recap, you have two basic roads into creating dramatic irony in any story. You can consciously go after the four emotional foundations (curiosity, anticipation, apprehension, anxiety—and their associated feelings) and design scenes that deliver those emotions in the proper dramatic context, or you can define the position of the reader vis-a-vis the POV character in any scene (equal, superior, inferior) to determine whether mystery or suspense is the best framework to apply to the scene. A stated earlier, one road is not better than the other, they are merely different roads.

SUMMARY

Narrative drive is part of the DNA and connective tissue of any well-told story. It is also an essential tool in the overall toolkit for any writer looking to achieve commercial pace in their fiction. Narrative drive finds its expression in the mechanical pacing strategies of writing style, chapter design, and manuscript design, but it is also found in the beats, scenes, story milestones, and significant story structure elements in any story. It's everywhere; in everything. But if it is missing or weak, then it will be missing everywhere in a story, and the mechanics of overall pacing will falter. Those mechanics (see chapter two, "The Structure of Pace") alone, however, will not be able to right a listing boat; you need narrative drive.

CONCLUSION

Commercial pace is part craft, part talent, part instinct, and part savvy sales and marketing. Simply put: commercial pace sells more books. Armed with the basic tools, strategies, and techniques listed in this e-book, you can consciously build stories that engage readers, hold them, and then move them through any level of narrative complexity to a satisfying ending.

Regardless of whether you are writing a book for print, online, or audio formats, the concepts outlined here will set you up for writing success. Your readers will keep coming back for more, and you will have a lot more fun writing and telling stories.

Commercial pace is one more tool for your storyteller's toolbox and one that can set you apart from most of your fellow writers out there in the growing world of indie authors and author-preneurs.

THE END

PART II

RAPID STORY DEVELOPMENT #2: BUST THE TOP TEN CREATIVE WRITING MYTHS TO BECOME A BETTER WRITER

THE TOP TEN CREATIVE WRITING MYTHS

We live in the age of clickbait, sound bites, and viral memes. On any given day, hour, minute, or second on Twitter, Facebook, or Instagram you can find any number of cat videos or fortune cookie platitudes meant to bolster one or another emotional cliché or bubble gum bromide. They reflect our moods and emotional states, reinforce happy thoughts, or confirm our darkest vulnerabilities. We read them, consume them, have a laugh or a wistful shrug of self-reflection, and move on to the next one, invariably saying to ourselves, "Oh, I'll have to remember that one," but we never do —it's always in one ear, out the other.

But, sometimes these little fortune cookies linger and gnaw at us, and ultimately solidify into calcified truisms. These insipid notions, memes, and banalities take on a substance they were never meant to have, and as a result often find a level of acceptance that far outweighs any implied "truth" they may hold, and so they endure and endure, eventually taking on an almost mythic significance (e.g., the ten "myths" below).

This phenomenon is everywhere, in all endeavors of creative life, but it is most easily seen in the world of creative writing where, for many, clichés have become the lifeblood of the creative process. "So what?" comes the obvious reaction. Who cares? Buying into the big myths and clichés of creative writing hasn't done any real harm; people keep writing, books and screenplays are still being published and produced, more creative writing is happening now than at any time in human history—so what's the big deal?

The big deal is that lots of harm follow these myths and clichés: wasted time, pointless writing, lost money, unnecessary struggle, missed opportunities, just-plain-bad writing, the list goes on. When you buy into these myths and memes, you go on creative autopilot and shut down the greatest gifts you have as a creative person: your ability to discern, your ability to assess, and your ability to make informed creative decisions. Abandoning the myths of creative writing is essential to maturing your creative and practical writing processes—and is at the heart of being a conscious writer.

WHAT IS A CONSCIOUS WRITER AND WHY SHOULD YOU CARE?

Before we look at the myths in question, it is crucial to understand what busting these myths really means. This e-book is not about ranting at the creative writing community about pet peeves and sour grapes. As I said earlier, I am convinced that these myths do incredible harm to creatives (not just writers) and are responsible for derailing many a creative process. But, complaining without offering solutions is nothing more than, well, whining.

That's why we have to talk about conscious writing and being a conscious writer, because being awake, having intentionality, being one's own agent is the exact opposite of what we are when we listen to the consensus creative writing community and blindly obey the myths and memes. We are at the farthest point possible from mastering our creative process when we drink the Kool-Aid or follow the gurus, or generally give our creative power away to some cleverly written Facebook creative writing meme involving cute puppies.

Because that is the heart of the matter: giving away our creative choice and power to some anonymous "other" for the cheap hit that comes from quick fixes and fast promises. The term is "snake oil," and the world of creative writing is slick and slippery with it.

THE SEVEN QUALITIES OF A CONSCIOUS WRITER:

- They intentionally make narrative choices based on creative objectives and goals; they do not stumble in the story dark, tripping into a story clueless how they got there.

- They know what they are writing, why they are writing it, and how they want to write it.
- They are always open to new approaches to storytelling and creative writing, and never dogmatic about any one approach.
- They are so steeped in the fundamentals of story development, and the best practices of creative writing that whenever they choose to stray from those fundamentals and best practices they do so with sure footedness, creative poise, and confidence in their craft.
- They listen to everyone, try everything, but follow no one; they are their own guru.
- They take responsibility for their failures as well as their successes and know that they (not some fortune cookie) are the only ones who can solve their writing problems—and they love that responsibility.
- They don't give their creative power away to anyone or anything—ever.

Being a conscious writer honors our true creative process and is the only path to achieve deep, authentic, and meaningful connection with readers. That's why busting the biggest myths of creative writing has got to rank as one of the most critical first steps on the road to becoming a conscious writer.

HOW WE WILL PROCEED

The best way to tackle this problem of myths, memes, and dumb advice is to break things down clearly into digestible pieces. It's not enough to have me rant and wail into the wind about how much I dislike one or another myth. No, you need me to do what I'm preaching to the choir: discern, assess, and offer choice. The very qualities of the conscious writer are required here to make a convincing argument while showing you the real impact and consequences of what will happen if you slip on that creative writing snake oil.

To help us navigate through this slimy path, I will break down each myth into four components: the lie, the truth, the danger, and the busting. *The lie* will be a clear statement of the myth, along with common judgements that are often associated with the myth. *The truth* will be a definite reality check demonstrating why the lie is a lie and what the reality of the myth is. *The danger* is the cautionary tale warning you of what consequences await if you choose to buy into the mythology, and *the busting* will explain the common sense writing strategies that you can use to break free of the lie and take back your creative power. So, let's take that first step here and now, and bust the top ten myths of creative writing.

TOP TEN MYTHS IN CREATIVE WRITING

(in reverse order of destructiveness)

#*10*: *Show don't tell.*

The lie: If you are not writing visual scenes, or giving the reader a visual experience, then you are failing. Telling is always inferior to showing action on the page. Lazy writers "tell," and successful writers "show."

The truth: It's not either/or, it's both. You must tell and show. Telling is called exposition. Showing is giving a visual expression to character behavior. The implied sub-lie here is that exposition is not your friend, so you should avoid it as much as possible. Not true. Exposition is a tool, and you must learn how to wield it effectively. Showing is not always the best solution or the right tool for the job.

Take a simple example: the teenage geek who is put under the tutelage of the grizzled martial arts master, whose job it is to turn the geek into a ninja killer—and he has 15 years to do the task. The 15 years that pass cannot be shown to the reader in detail—it would take an entire book to show how the boy or girl goes from geek to killer. Showing in this situation is not the best writing tool in the toolbox. This situation calls for showing. The kid's transformation must be told in exposition, but cut down to a manageable amount of prose.

Showing, in this case, would be pacing death to any story. No, you use telling exposition to economically reduce the 15 years down to a few paragraphs, or maybe a few pages, and then you move on to the mainline story with a minimal digression. But telling doesn't mean you are only giving information, delivering facts, or filling in story gaps between visual moments.

Telling can also be setting the mood; establishing emotional context; and building the inner life of a character through emotions, thoughts, and ideas. This is all exposition/telling, and often this is the preferred form of prose tool for the job at hand. In the movie world, the tool for doing this is called the montage. Screenwriters splice together a series of shots (usually a few) to demonstrate the passing of time and the evolution of the change taking place, then jump back into the mainline story after the montage. Prose writers can do the same thing with well-written exposition.

Writers tell all the time; we have to tell a lot, sometimes more than we show. The key is knowing when to do one versus the other. This is where the abilities of the conscious writer mentioned earlier come into play. You have to *discern* the context, *assess* the purpose of the scene, and make an informed *decision* what best serves your purposes as a writer. If you are on autopilot, you will blindly follow the myth and miss the opportunity of writing the best scenes possible.

The danger: The danger of this myth is that your writing will lack substance and risk leaving too little on the writing table. There are things that dialogue and set pieces can't convey alone. Giving your reader strategically selected facts or backstory through exposition, in the right places in the story, can make or break the subtly or power of accompanying action or dialogue. It's the either-or mindset that is the villain here, not the favoring of one technique over the other.

How to bust it: Screenwriters typically don't have a problem with this. Keeping exposition under control is a given in screenwriting, and only amateurs make the mistake of writing many paragraphs of text exposition in scripts. Brief, essential descriptions and the use of montages usually get the job done leaving any script readable and looking professional.

Novelists, however, are not so fortunate. The whole culture of fiction writing encourages exposition, and seldom imposes constraints, or establishes useful boundaries to help prose writers develop a clear sense of when they are meandering and losing focus. If you're writing a so-called literary work and could care less about page count, pacing, or whether anyone is buying your books, then by all means, ignore this advice, and enjoy yourself and meander to your heart's content. But, if commercial fiction and and genre writing is your game, then you would do well to take a screenwriter's approach to showing and telling.

Learn as much as you can about the screenwriting technique of the montage (a series of short shots edited into a sequence to condense space, time, and information) and then adapt it to long-form prose writing. There is a wonderful scene from season two of *The West Wing* (Warner Bros. Television, 1999) in which the White House Counsel, Oliver Babish (Oliver Platt), asks the White House Press Secretary, C.J. Cregg (Allison Janney), "Do you know what time it is?" C.J. responds with the time. Babish coolly tells her, "I'd like you to get out of the habit of doing that." C.J. is miffed, "Doing what?" Babish says, "Answering more than was asked." Get yourself out of the habit of writing more than is asked by the scene, chapter, or story by teaching yourself that less is more and that you can often accomplish in two paragraphs what many authors drag on for two pages. "Think like a screenwriter" is probably the best advice I can think of to practically help you to unlearn the consensus bad habits of contemporary fiction and creative nonfiction writing.

#9: The blank page is the enemy.

The lie: When you sit in front of the blank page (or screen) you are in for pain and anxiety and angst. The blank page will resist any attempts to fill it, and it is your biggest obstacle.

The truth: It's just a piece of paper. It's a blank word processing document. Get a grip. The "obstacle" is not the blank whatever, the obstacle is your head—or more correctly what's inside your head. This myth ties into the #5 myth about writer's block, because this and #5 have to do with having so much going on in your head that you can't prioritize and order your creative process enough to be productive. You are so jumbled and crowded with ideas that you can't break the logjam. The truth is: nature abhors a vacuum, including the blank page. Filling it is easy; filling with the best content, however, is a whole other e-book.

The danger: The danger of buying into this myth is that it conditions you to give your power away to some inanimate object (piece of paper or blank screen), and hold that "other" responsible for your inability to be productive. It doesn't have the power, you do. Clear the mind, clear the logjam, order your creative thought process and the ideas will flow, because they are there—you have to get out of their way. More on how to do this in #5.

How to bust it: This one is far from rocket science; it's a quick reality check. Look down at the table and piece of paper in front of you (or across to the blank monitor) and tell yourself, "It's a blank space—that's it." No big deal, no magical mojo needed, no sacrificing of animals, etc. Just start typing or writing something and voila—no longer an empty page. Problem solved.

This is not meant to be flippant or disregarding of your anxiety in the face of blankness. On the contrary, this is intended to offer a straightforward action that breaks the trance of the mythology, and thus free you to act. Once you are in action, it is a simple matter to keep going.

#8: *Write what you know.*

The lie: If you can only write what you know, then you will be limited and constricted in what you can write. Writing what you know is restricted by your own life experience, and if you only know your life then how boring will your writing be?

The truth: This myth is a very good piece of writing advice, but people get the purpose of it all wrong. Writing what you know isn't about writing things that happened (necessarily), it is about writing the emotional content of what happened in your life. If you felt abused, write what you know about that. If you felt loved, write about that. If you felt afraid, write about that. The actual events might be part of that, but it's what's under the emotional hood that will grab readers—and only you can write about that from your own emotional experience. This is what makes your writing relatable to readers because readers who felt abused or loved, or afraid growing up will relate accordingly. The other truth here is that you can't write about stuff you don't know. In other words, you are forced by circumstance (i.e., life itself) to only write what you, because you don't know what you don't know. Even if you make everything up in a story, that fiction can only be sourced from what you know—as a writer you have no other experience other than your life experience. So, writing what you know is unavoidable, but it is also important to be reminded of the truth of the sentiment.

The danger: The danger of the myth is that misinterpreting the meaning of the advice can artificially restrict or constrict your ability to write. If you can only write what you know, then you will be constrained in what you can write. As stated earlier, writing what you know is bounded by your own life experience. If you are a secret agent and have a license to kill, then you have an exciting experience to write about. But, if you hand out tokens on the New Jersey Parkway, how boring is your writing going to be? And here is the danger: assuming the happenings of your life are the things you should be writing about. No, not the events, but the emotions. Even James Bond felt love (after a fashion), the same love as any token-taker on the Parkway.

How to bust it: Focus on two ideas, firstly: I'm not writing about what I know; I'm writing about what I feel. Secondly, think about: Emotion exists outside of time and space, so I can write about the past, present, or future and I know enough to do that. These two simple ideas reframe the myth so that it sets you up for success and not failure (or immediate self-judgement that you're not enough). Repeat these two ideas over and over until they are second nature, and you will never worry about whether you are writing what you know; you will just do it.

#7: *Real writers write every day.*

The lie: The best way to be productive and accomplish success is always to exercise the "writing muscle," so that means never losing momentum—write every day.

The truth: No, writers don't write every day. This myth ties into the #1 myth of "just do it." Just keep writing, because that's what writers do. It also feeds into the next myth about story-telling versus writing (you can see how all these myths actually reinforce one another and can thus derail you as they gang up on your creative process). The truth here is you don't have to write every day. I'm not sure who made this rule up, but it is total hooey. Other than eating, sleeping, and going to the bathroom there are few things we must do every day. Writing is certainly not on that list.

The fact is, most writers are not writing every day, and because they buy into this dumb myth they beat themselves up and feel guilty because they're not writing. But they are doing something else (probably every day): they are thinking about writing and thinking about story. So much happens when we writers stop writing and mull over ideas (I certainly do). Thinking about writing, especially thinking about story, are more important than writing because it is what gives fuel to the writing process.

It's called story development, and this is something writers do almost daily and certainly more often than physical writing. Be clear; I am not poo-pooing physically writing. I'm putting it in perspective with other forms of creative process that help you get the words on the page.

The danger: The danger of this myth is that it might make a writer discount their internal story development process as less valuable than the act of physical writing. Just the opposite is true. If you write every day, fine, have at it. But, know that doing so doesn't make you more of a writer, or even make you more productive as a writer. The writer that thinks and ponders story development more than physically writing is probably going to produce more useful work product than the one that blindly writes every day hoping for real productivity (because that's what writers are supposed to do).

How to bust it: Give yourself a break! Get off your own back. Please believe me when I say that the writing gods are not standing over you with a clipboard marking off each day you fail to write with a big, black "X." There are no writing gods, and there are no clipboards. But there is your ego pestering you to measure up, do it right, be a good boy-girl and do what everyone else does. Tell the little voice to go away and shut up and pester someone else. You have better things to do, like think about your stories. Plan your stories. Talk to your characters when you're driving in your car or research the rich worlds you are trying to create on paper.

Writing a book and telling a story are complex activities requiring many skills, talents, and subject matter knowledge.

Writing is the one activity that pulls all the other work into place and is thus the unifying factor, but when you view the writing function as part of an even bigger whole, then the writing is like any other piece. You won't do every piece every day; you can't. You don't have enough hours in the day. So, you find your flow, your workflow, your process for development and writing and you write when it's time, not because someone hits you with a clipboard. The key to busting this one is perspective. Keep your writing in perspective in relation to the massive job you have of creating a piece of narrative prose.

#6: *Storytelling and writing are the same thing.*

The lie: Writing is storytelling and storytelling is writing. There is no difference, and any perceived difference is semantics.

The truth: Storytelling and writing are two different things, and they have nothing to do with one another. Storytelling is about story. Storytelling is about us. Story is what we tell ourselves about what it means to be human. We've been telling ourselves stories for 40-thousand-plus years. We've only been writing for 6 or 7 thousand years. Writing, on the other hand, is about language/rhetoric; it is about the rhythm and musicality of using language to convey meaning, thoughts, and ideas.

There is nothing that intrinsically connects writing to story-telling. Storytelling preceded writing, and a story doesn't need to be anywhere near the written word in order to be told. Think about it; stories can be: danced, mimed, painted, sculpted, sung, spoken—or written. Stories need storytellers, not writers. This is a hard one for people to wrap their heads around, especially if they think writing is storytelling. No, writing is only one way to render a story.

In addition, because they (writing and storytelling) are separate phenomena, they also represent separate kinds of talent and separate kinds of skill sets. Because you are good at one does not mean you will be good at the other. In fact, most writers are good at the writing function, but bad or poor at the story function. Storytelling is usually not the strongest skill set with most writers. This is why learning story structure and story development craft is so critically important for creative writers.

The danger: The danger of buying into this myth is that writers will assume because they can string two sentences together, and turn a nice phrase, they can tell a story properly. The myth gives them a false sense of security in their own skill sets and talents. Writers must learn how to do both well, that means learning the craft of story development and the craft of creative writing. Read that last sentence again.

How to bust it: Learn story. That's how you break the hold of this myth. It is that straightforward. I discuss in some depth this issue of writing versus storytelling in my book *Anatomy of a Premise Line* (Focal Press, 2015). The entire book is focused on the principles of story development, not creative writing. There is no substitute for learning craft—none. And there is no excuse not to learn it.

There are hundreds of books, videos, classes *ad nauseam* available to help you with this task. Find a guru, teacher, master, or some guy or gal who you like that teaches story structure and learn it. After you understand what they have to teach, thank them and move on to the next one. Keep going until you feel you have a solid foundation in story development and story structure. That's as simple and as complicated as has to get. I'm not going to recommend any one guru (not even me), suffice to say you will have to kiss a lot of frogs before you find your prince. It's a lot like finding a good therapist; you keep testing them out until you resonate with one. You will find them! And when you do, you will then understand how story and writing are two different activities that have nothing to do with one another, but when they do get combined, magic can happen.

#5: *Writer's block is real.*

The lie: Duh—writer's block is real.

The truth: No, it is not (well, kind of). What most people perceive as writer's block isn't writer's block, it's only a generic blockage. What I mean is this: the feeling of being blocked has nothing to do with the writing process. A writer might feel blocked because their lover left them, or they have financial trouble, or life has them depressed—and while this might affect their ability to write, the blockage itself has nothing to do with writing or creative process. The solution to the blockage is also unrelated to the writing process (i.e., find a new lover, get a job, get therapy). In other words: writer's block is only valid if it sources from your writing process, and there is only *one* circumstance where this might occur—when you have so much in your creative pipeline that you can't prioritize and make informed creative choices what to do next.

That is blockage related to the actual writing process, and thus the only legitimate form of writer's block. I have written extensively on this issue (*Anatomy of a Premise Line: How to Master Premise and Story Development for Writing Success*, Focal Press 2015), but the bottom line is that any blockage that is not related to this single issue (pipeline too clogged) is not writer's block, it is merely a life blockage. The solution to this legitimate form (and only form) of writer's block is directly related to writing process: i.e., apply your craft and story structure skills to break the blockage. A writing problem (blockage) needs a writing solution.

Getting therapy, or taking a yoga class, or going to watch TV, or walking in the forest is not going to work. I repeat: *writing problems require writing solutions*. This is why I say writer's block is 99.9 per cent smoke and .1 per cent substance. The .1 per cent is the only part you can do anything about.

The danger: The danger of this myth is that, as with myth #3, writers give their creative power away to some mysterious "other" that is controlling their process and productivity. The block has them in its hold, it's not something the writer can control at will. The writer has to wait for the block to break up, or pass, or—. In the meantime, lots of time is spent walking on beaches, or taking yoga classes, or drinking wine, or watching CNN, or pick a distraction. None of those activities is bad and wrong in and of themselves, but in the context of writer's block they are distractions, not solutions or productive strategies to get writing, and therein lies the danger.

How to bust it: I devote the entire last chapter of my book *Anatomy of a Premise Line* to this topic and offer a 7-step strategy for busting writer's block. You can go to my website and download that chapter for free as an e-book sample chapter, or you can take a yoga class—your call. My biggest challenge in giving advice on how to bust this myth is that people take the idea of writer's block very personally. When I suggest that writer's block is 99.9 percent bunk people get very defensive and push back as if I've attacked their integrity.

After all, here I am invalidating their emotional experience. They feel blocked and I'm saying the block is smoke and mirrors. Who the heck am I to tell them what they should feel? And they are correct. I have no right to do that, and that is not my intention. My suggestion to anyone feeling blocked is that they consider the source: if the block is from inside them and the story, then this is great news—*writing problems require writing solutions*—go to your story structure and see where you are getting hung up and write through it. This always works.

But, if the block is coming from outside of you, i.e., from life getting in the way and affecting your writing, then deal with that. Get therapy, get help, do what you have to do to get the life blockage out of the way so you can get back to your own life. One is writing-related; the other is life-related. They both require different strategies to clear. That is my point. Remember about being a conscious writer? Know what is happening; assess, discern, be informed then make a plan and act. Take back your power and know that being "blocked" from time to time is merely a part of the normal story development process, not some writing road hazard that you will drive over, stalling out your car. Falling back on your story structure craft skills is the royal road to busting writer's block and freeing your productivity, in fact, it is the only way to clear the pipeline and get writing again.

#4: There are no rules when it comes to creative writing.

The lie: Nobody knows anything (as screenwriter William Goldman once said). There are no rules to creative writing, so don't get distracted by all the how-to experts out there. Just write.

The truth: Of course, there are rules. The universe runs on rules. Physics has rules, and chemistry has rules, mathematics has rules. How does creative writing get a pass on that? Of course, there are rules, and those rules are the rules of classical story structure and the established rules of language usage (grammar, syntax, and rhetoric). Rules run everything based on a system—the physical universe dictates this, not story or writing gurus. So, who says what the story structure or language rules should be? This gets a bit problematic, I understand, but this isn't hard to figure out.

Every so-called story expert or creative writing teacher teaches the same basic stuff. Yes, they all have their proprietary theories and ideas that they slap on lunch pails and market so they can pay the rent, but at the core of every guru's "teachings" are the same basic concepts. It doesn't take a rocket scientist to figure those out, but it does take getting familiar with what is being taught "out there," and then using those conscious-writer abilities I talked about in #10 to discern the universal truths of story or writing. As Picasso said, "Learn the rules like a pro so you can break them like an artist." There are rules to storytelling, and there are rules to great writing and learning them is part of the craft of storytelling and creative writing.

The danger: The danger of buying into the "no rules" approach is that writers think they can fly free, unhindered by best practices, and everything will work out. This is another form of giving away one's power to the process, rather than taking responsibility for it. Learn your craft, learn the rules, then break them like a conscious writer.

How to bust it: The solution to this myth is similar to some of the others mentioned: learn craft. Mastering the basics of writing and story craft is essential. Take pride in your technical knowledge. Become a grammar snob, know punctuation, understand proper syntax and style rules for English (or whatever language you write in) and continuously expand your technical understanding, so you master the tools of your craft. Writers who ignore the rules of grammar, or who never understand the proper usage of lay vs lie, or the rules for the Oxford comma, or ignore the standards established by the bible of the publishing industry *The Chicago Manual of Style* run the risk of being perpetual amateurs lacking real professional competence.

What does it say about your commitment to your art when you take a lackluster attitude toward the nuts-and-bolts of basic craft? And how will you be regarded by publishing professionals when your work shows weak skill sets? So, learn the rules so you can break them like an artist.

#3: *Good stories and good characters write themselves.*

The lie: Good stories will talk to you and take over, and you will be led by the story, rather than forcing it yourself. When this happens, it will feel effortless and flow smoothly and you will be in the zone. So, get out of the way and let the story find its voice and expression.

The truth: Stories don't write themselves and characters don't write themselves. You are the writer; you write it all—it's all you and your subconscious mind. When you are in sync with your subconscious mind, and with your creative process, it will feel effortless, easy, and flowing. You will be in the zone. But, it is not the story driving the process, it is you. I state again: You are the writer. You are in control, but that doesn't mean you are being controlling. Being in control doesn't mean dominating and containing and forcing. Being in control means harnessing, directing, and co-creating with your creative process. Buying into this myth is another form of giving away your power to the process itself, rather than taking total responsibility for it.

Ironically this is one of the reasons writers fear the blank page because they sit waiting for the story to take control and tell them where to go. When that doesn't happen, they get anxious and often despairing, "Why isn't the story talking to me?" Well, it's not talking because you're not giving it anything to say! You're its voice, not the other way around. It might feel that way when you're in that zone but be very clear, "in the zone" means you are in sync with your creativity and in balance with your talent and craft, and when these are in balance your process will flow elegantly and fluidly and feel as if it is running by itself with you trailing behind. It may feel that way, but that is not what is happening. You are the creative force, not the story and not the characters. You, the writer, give the story its form and its characters their voices. Never forget this: don't ever give away your power, not even to your own stories.

The danger: The danger should be a familiar one by now, as it rings true for several other of these myths. The great danger is that the writer will sit down to write and sit back waiting for the muse, or the milkman, or whoever it is that brings the inspiration. And while they wait, the negative yammer-yammer of the negative ego starts to bubble up and with it doubt, confusion, frustration, and ultimately self-judgement that freezes them in place—and kiss that writing session goodbye. This is the epitome of what it means to give away your creative power to the process.

How to bust it: Tell yourself the truth: you are the writer and, you direct the show. Get confused, get frustrated, get angry, but know it's all you all the time. We carry out processes, not the other way around. We tell stories, they don't tell us. This is the key to busting this myth: you as the writer are the source, the

82

inspiration, and the execution. Inspiration doesn't come as a function of waiting; it is a function of writing. You are the writer.

#2: *Outlines and story structure kill creativity.*

The lie: Outlining, planning, and structuring are all too controlling of the story. When you do these things, you limit yourself and kill the creative process, which has to flow unfettered to be most effective. Be a pantser (go with the flow, by the seat of your pants), not a planner.

The truth: Just the opposite is true. Story development and creative writing are reductive processes, not additive. What this means is that as you develop your story you have to make choices: make Joe the hero, set the story in New York, make the genre sci-fi, give Joe a love interest, etc. Likewise, you make writing decisions: tell the story in the first person, use flashbacks, keep chapters under three pages, etc.

Every choice you make reduces your options and limits your set of resources that you can draw on for scene-level material. If you choose A, then you eliminate B through Z. Development and writing reduce your options, they do not increase them, but this opens up your creativity because you have direction and form and structure that all work together to generate new ideas and possible scene material. And those new ideas are all in harmony with the choices you have made, so everything holds together dramatically and is internally consistent.

If you hadn't made those choices you would constantly be sifting through irrelevant options and bad choices, thus making your work harder and the process torturous. In other words, development is planning, outlining, and structuring. Every writer does it, even the ones who say they don't.

For example you choose scene A over scene B. Okay, what do you do next? You think about it and have to decide what comes next, what is scene C? Okay, what makes sense? So, you look at scene A and figure out what preceded scene A, i.e., why does scene A make sense and how does it lead to scene B? Because scene C has to be consistent with both other scenes. Even if it's only three scenes deep, you're outlining your story. Keep going every three scenes like that, and you'll end up with a book or screenplay. It's not about how many scenes deep you go, it's the function of what you are doing—you're outlining/planning. Everyone does this, everyone. And this frees you to be more creative, not less creative, because it quiets the chaos of unlimited choices, so that you can see the trees for the forest.

The danger: The great danger of buying into this myth is that you end up devaluing and dismissing being organized and disciplined as a writer. There are zero professional novelists I know who do not plan their novels to some extent, including using outlines. They may not follow those outlines, but the part that outlines help them with—prioritizing and selecting what is or is not working—is a benefit gleaned from their outlining process. Only amateurs fly by the seat of their word processors expecting the magical writing muses to do the heavy lifting for them.

But, there are enough of these kinds of people out there to give legs to this myth—thus the warning. As stated above, planning and organizing your work is essential, not antithetical to creativity. Creativity has boundaries and constraints, like anything else. If it were boundless and limitless and infinitely expansive then you would never get any work done—you would be lost in imagination with no direction or purpose. It is the creative choices you make during the creative process that define the boundaries of your imagination and thus make it possible for you to move from idea to idea productively. How obsessive-compulsive you get about your organization is the subject of another kind of e-book, but for our purposes here, planning, not pantsing, is your friend.

How to bust it: This is one of the easiest myths to bust. All it takes is treating your writing projects like any other project. Develop a workflow and process procedures that you can carry over from book to book. This includes the nuts-and-bolts activities of organizing your office, research methods, filing system, and other back-office procedures, but it also includes your writing workflow: how you write, edit, and document your development process. It's a matter of taking the time to develop these strategies, and to then test them as you go to see which ones support or hinder your creative process and overall productivity.

#1: *Just do it. Just write.*

The truth: This is, without doubt, the single most harmful piece of writing advice ever conceived. Yes, everyone's first draft is crap, but it can be good crap versus bad crap. Buying into this myth almost universally results in failed writing; voluminous pages of useless manuscripts; despair and depression; and huge sums of money lost in the form of wasted writing time, or third-party services hired to fix the voluminous pages. Writers who fall prey to this advice almost always end up lost in the story woods, or drowning in the story floodplain. I say, "Almost always," because there is a small subset of writers who appear able to "just do it." These are the writers who are naturally gifted and talented with what I call the story gene. They intuitively know story structure and can naturally avoid getting lost in the development woods, but they don't know how they do it. They are not aware of what is saving them.

Savant-like, they instinctively know what not to do, and so stay on track. They are often the ones who are most vocal about "just doing it," because it works for them, so why shouldn't everyone else? These are the rare few who are born with the storytelling gift. Most writers are not so lucky, consequently "just do it" is a recipe for disaster. Missing the story gene, most writers have to shore up their story development craft skills the old-fashioned way: practice, practice, practice. But, once strengthened, writers can successfully navigate the development and writing processes with less fear of getting lost in the woods, and whatever first draft they end up with will be more structurally sound and cohesive as a narrative—thus making the rewrite process much more productive. But, getting to the point where a writer understands their vulnerabilities concerning this myth is often a painful process.

The danger: The danger is clear: "just writing" is disastrous for writers who do not have a natural ability to sense story (i.e., have the story gene). They will get lost in the story woods and waste countless hours, weeks, or months writing themselves into blind alleys and dark corners. If you are twenty years old, okay, maybe you don't mind the lost time and energy. But, if you're fifty, do you have the time to waste going off into story limbo? I don't think so. Getting back on track is painful, time-consuming, and often treacherous.

How to bust it: This is where becoming a conscious writer can save your creative life; so, hone your abilities of assessment, discernment, and informed choice. Learn that story structure is your personal superpower, and story development is your closest friend. The evil villain is writing blindly at the service of some twisted definition of creativity, not the patience that comes from story development. Once again, it is about being in control of your creative process, not being controlled by it.

CONCLUSION

The toolbox of conventional—and oh-so-generic— creative writing advice is chock full of easy to digest placeboes that will soothe a writer's nerves and calm shaky confidence. Sadly, any palliative effects don't last long, and the pesky shakes always return, usually with a vengeance.

The solution to lasting relief is not more sound bites and

bromides, but rather information, critical thinking, and trust in your creative process. Do not listen to these ten sirens (myths) bewitching you toward the rocks, because they will only seduce you to your doom with their promise of quick fixes and feel-good stopgaps.

Tapping your ability to assess, discern, and make creative choice based on being a conscious writer is the only long-term solution to the anxieties and angst that are unavoidable in the creative writing process. Don't ever give your creative power away to anyone, or anything, and certainly not to the myths of creative writing.

THE END

HONORABLE MENTION: MYTH #11

ATTACK OF THE THREE-ACT STRUCTURE

Many creative writing myths qualified for the top-ten list you just reviewed, but the chosen finalists were the ones I felt were the most destructive—and the most widely accepted by writers. There was one myth that kept coming up as a popular choice among the writers whom I interviewed during the writing of this e-book. This eleventh myth was wildly popular and commonly held as "truth" by almost everyone, regardless of the form of their writing (novels, nonfiction, or screenplays). Screenwriters were especially adamant about this particular myth, more so than novelists. I'm talking about the idea that stories are told in three acts, and that three acts is a useful construct for writing any story. Three acts, according to the myth, is essential for writing any story, because all stories have three act.

I struggled with whether or not to include three-act structure in the final list of top-ten, but I decided that the other myths were more universally known. Even so, the three-act construct is so pervasive and so widely accepted as valid that it demanded at least an honorable mention.

I want to give this myth a bit more detailed treatment, however, than a quick summary and review like the earlier ten. The reason for this is that the idea of three acts is so ubiquitous in the creative writing world that it needs to be put in proper perspective, both historically as a phenomenon, and technically as a tool for writers, to be fully appreciated as the creative writing snake oil it truly is.

WHAT IS IT ABOUT ACTS?

Whether it's three, five, six, or seven acts, it doesn't matter. "Acts" are all useless to writers—as storytellers. For many, when they hear me say this with such certainty—with such sureness—they feel it is pure bravado and arrogance on my part. After all, no one should know anything with the level of finality that I display when I say, "Acts are useless to writers." So, what gives me such a sure hand in this game? Why don't I want to give up some of the moral high ground to the possibility that I might be wrong? Am I, in fact, wrong? Many will think so, even after reading this e-book.

But, I would suggest that the strength of my conviction about this issue is not due to ego run amok, or some other petty agenda. No, my sureness about rejecting three-act structure sources from writing itself—indeed, from writing process, story development, and storytelling. Look at who tends to be the most vulnerable when it comes to falling prey to this insidious writing myth: i.e., new writers or writers who have little or no exposure to narrative theory, story development best practices, or classic story structure principles. But, even experienced writers can slip down this mythological slope.

A perfect example of this is the industry town of Hollywood, where this notion of three acts has taken hold like a spiteful weed. To this day, at the highest levels of creative power, creative executives all talk about three acts. You can hardly "take a meeting" with anyone without hearing this phrase uttered, or being asked to deliver a three-act screenplay.

Not to point fingers, because I think the actual origin of the use of three acts today is impossible to "finger," but one influential source was Syd Field, the renown and revered "father" of the screenwriting consulting and how-to industry. We all have a debt of gratitude to this man for trailblazing the field of screen-writing for popular audiences. He was a great man, and he deserves his place in the pantheon of screenwriting marketing mavericks. Yeah, I know ... here comes the "but."

But—Syd, more than anyone else, popularized the idea of three acts through his "paradigm" theory; the idea that stories are told in three acts, and that the second act should be broken up into parts A and B. And because he was "the first," and because he was articulate and made sense, people assumed this must be true; this must be the way of things. Hollywood (and not just Hollywood) swallowed three-act structure hook, line, and sinker. In short, three-act structure became a given; it was assumed to be part of the normal writing process. It is a meme that is almost universally unquestioned and accepted as chapter-and-verse of the writing how-to bible.

WHERE DID "ACTS" COME FROM?

Way back in the days of the Greeks, we're talking circa 500–300 B.C.—drama was king. Theater, in the form of epic poetry, was the Comic-Con of the age. Physical plays performed by human beings on a stage that required moving sets and technical setups (some amazingly elaborate) were an unavoidable part of physical production of a play. Even then it was not thought smart to have the audience sit and watch the sausage being made, so some enterprising Greek came up with the idea of curtains or screens that could be put into place to shield the audience from the gross happenings between scene transitions. Curtains were one way not to break the mood, to not lose the dramatic tempo, etc.

Thus, acts were born. Writers started writing to accommodate these changes in the physical staging requirements of their plays. Acts were sometimes one, two, three, or even ten! Even twenty-five hundred years ago there was no hard and fast rule about the number three. So, the concept of acts is not an idea related to telling a story; it is an idea associated with a specific form of delivering a story: i.e., a staged performance. Acts are about the constraints of physical stage production and delivery, not writing or storytelling.

Beyond theater, commercial television (or radio—yes, it still exists) is the only other place where acts make sense, because of commercials. Every 17 or 20 minutes you have to break the story to advertise—thus an act break. TV shows have anywhere from 4–6 acts due to commercial requirements. Again, not a part of storytelling, but rather a consequence of selling soap, i.e., how the story is delivered due to the constraints of the story-telling environment! (Remember, TV is not an entertainment medium, it is a sales medium— commercial TV shows exist so you'll watch the commercials, not the other way around.)

And don't blame Aristotle (384–322 B.C.) He is often cited as the first person to talk about acts in theater in his foundational work Poetics, where he supposedly laid out the necessity of using acts in drama and comedy." WRONG! Aristotle talked about a beginning, middle and end in any drama or comedy, but he laid down no such rules about acts.

"But, Shakespeare himself used act. All his plays were five acts. Surely that's proof that acts are important," comes the plaintive cry. Actually, wrong again. Shakespeare didn't divide his plays into acts. That was first done "for him" by playwright Nicholas Rowe (1674–1718) in his six-volume edition of Shakespeare's plays published in 1709. If Shakespeare were alive today, he would laugh if he opened a copy of one of his plays to see acts of any number. So, what happened? Why five acts? Was there something particularly English about the number five? Well, kind of—something Roman. Elizabethan playwrights wrote in five acts because that was the meme of the time.

The tragedies of the great dramatist Lucius Annaeus Seneca (c. 4 BC–AD 65) were wildly popular in the 1600s, and Seneca's five-act structure, as well as his blood-thirsty themes, profoundly influenced Elizabethan dramatists. Shakespeare's peers all drank Seneca's Kool-Aid—with some great results. But, none of those results was because of five acts. So, you can't blame the Bard or his contemporaries for acts either.

There is no blame to be had in this examination. Acts are an artifact of ancient Greek theater production, one carried forward by dramatists and writers through aeons of imitation and brilliant writing. The issue is that in all this propagation of the past, with its memes, brilliant writers lost perspective on the true nature of this thing they loyally championed without ever asking the obvious question, "Is this necessary?"

We can easily forgive this oversight on the part of playwrights, as theater is theater and production is production. Acts make sense in theater. But, as entertainment forms evolved, acts lost their usefulness, except as a device for selling soap in commercial radio and TV. If there is blame to be had, we are all responsible for perpetuating this myth. And, as we are the ones responsible, we are the ones who can end it.

THE PACING PROBLEM

The only writing-related argument I have ever heard, that on the surface sounds reasonable and sane, as to why writers should use acts is the claim that many writers make, "I love the three-act structure because it helps me pace out a story." I have heard from many writers that without thinking about their stories broken into three or more parts, they would have a harder time putting the right pieces in the right places to get the best pace and flow for their narratives. I have to admit, this makes sense, like "Eat your peas," or "Wait half an hour to go in the water after eating a meal." It's good common sense, sound thinking, solid advice—and no more true than "The Earth is flat."

The pacing argument doesn't hold any practical water for the simple reason that arbitrary divisions of a screenplay or novel do nothing to pace a story. I address the issue of pacing in the first e-book in this series, *Rapid Story Development: Pacing in Fiction and Creative Nonfiction.* There I explain that pacing is a function of four essential foundation stones: writing style, chapter design, manuscript design, and narrative drive. I won't go into how these three areas work together to achieve commercial pace in a book, suffice to say that proper pacing is not a function of breaking a manuscript up into sections. It comes from how language is used, how chapters are engineered to maximum dramatic effect, and how the book itself is organized to maximize flow and execution of story structure elements.

But, with that said, I have to soften my stance a bit and give some of that high ground after all. Because, if three-acts is like a fuzzy blanket that you can't give up, and you are convinced that it is helping you write, then go for it. I say whatever gets you productive is worth continuing to use. If you find a perceived benefit in the act (no pun intended), who am I to tell you to stop? You're not bad or wrong for using three acts, you've just drunk the Kool-Aid—like so many of us. When you don't know any better, you do what seems to work, whether you know it will work or not, "Everybody else seems hot on this idea, so heck, I might as well go for it too." But, there is a better way than going along with the consensus—a way that is natural to writing and fully supportive of the writing process, not for selling soap or keeping butts in seats at the amphitheater.

STORY STRUCTURE IS THE SOLUTION

Story structure is where writers need to go to find writing solutions for writing problems. Every story has a structure; every story must have a structure. If it doesn't, then it is not a story; it is something else. Story structure works because it naturally reveals the right and proper flow for any narrative. Story structure gives you a natural beginning, middle, and end—and then it gives you the critical milestones along the way, showing you where to put the dramatic stakes, reversals, twists, high points, low points, character change points, and the final big-bang or big-whimper ending. Story structure paces out your story for you—naturally, using the story itself— without one, two, three, four, or any number of acts being needed.

CONCLUSION

It is beyond the scope of this e-book to detail specifically how story structure and commercial pace can all contribute to the proper flow of any story's narrative. There are many approaches "out there" in the how-to writing world offering solutions to the general problem of pacing and other general challenges facing writers regarding flow, tone, and narrative design, including my approaches (*Anatomy of a Premise Line, Rapid Story Development: Pacing in Fiction and Creative Nonfiction*).

None of these is better or worse than the others, in terms of principles taught, but some are more productive than others. My objective here, with the suggestion of this eleventh myth, is to bring this issue of acts (of however many numbers) into the light of critical examination. In that light, I hope you will apply the new principles you have learned here of the conscious writer: i.e., discernment, information, and choice. From this conscious position, you can then decide for yourself how you want to proceed with this question: follow the consensus or be your own guru. So, start kicking some story tires and test the various teachers out there. Listen to everyone, try everything; and pick an approach to story development that resonates with you as a writer. As long as the approach you choose doesn't rely on the concept of acts you will be better off than doing nothing at all—or worse, following the same-ol'-same-ol', cookie-cutter, three-act straightjacket.

THE END

PART III

RAPID STORY DEVELOPMENT #3: TEN QUESTIONS EVERY WRITER NEEDS TO ASK BEFORE THEY HIRE A CONSULTANT

WHAT AM I GETTING MYSELF INTO?

Whether you are a screenwriter, novelist, or creative nonfiction author, at some point in your writing career you will face the day when you decide you need help. Maybe the narrative wheels came off the cart, maybe you wrote yourself into a dead end, maybe you found yourself drowning in the story floodplains with no land in sight, or maybe you just want to get an opinion on your work that is not your mother's. Whatever the reason, you determine that hiring a third-party expert might be a smart move, and so you bite the bullet and hire a story consultant or an editor.

For most writers, this decision is fraught with confusion and uncertainty, "What do these consultants do anyway? How do I know they know what they're doing? What's the difference between a story consultant, line editor, and developmental editor?" Quickly you discover the editorial zoo is crowded, expensive, and intimidating, and you are not well-prepared to engage the zoo animals quite yet.

Unless you have been in the business world and have experienced hiring third-parties and vendors for contract work, you probably approach the problem of getting help the same way you do looking for a handyman when something breaks around the house or finding a good plumber, or computer tech when your computer crashes.

There are no contracts, no project plans, no schedule of deliverables, proposal requests, or review periods. You hire a person; they do the job, it gets done (or not), and you move on. If there is a dispute, you call up customer service and complain to a manager, or the manager's manager, and make a lot of noise until you get your money back (good luck with that). This is how most people approach editorial help with their scripts or prose fiction; what I call the consensus approach. Not bad or wrong, but not very professional, and not very smart from a cover-your-butt point of view.

If you find yourself falling into this consensus mindset on hiring third-parties, I would suggest that there is great benefit in changing this mindset and adopting a more business-like attitude. Especially if your long-term goal is creating a life for yourself as a working writer, building a reader base, and publishing a body of work that can support you over time, both creatively and financially.

EDITORIAL VS. WRITING EXPERIENCE

I have written a great deal on the distinction between story-telling and creative writing, explaining how they are unrelated and completely different talents and crafts. Many people are good writers, but not so good with story. It's important to know the degree to which this statement might be true for you as a writer. Are you weak on story development basics? Are you weak in creative writing skills? If the answer is yes to either of those questions, then you have some shoring up to do. If you are weak with story, then take some story structure classes, learn premise development, learn the basics of story. If you have a natural ability for story, but are weak in writing style, grammar, and rhetoric then take some classes on creative writing.

Everything I'm saying here about story development and creative writing is also true for editorial skills. It is critical to understand that being a good writer (or storyteller) and being a good editor or story consultant are two different things. Editorial talent and craft are not necessarily skills writers have in abundance. We all edit our own work from time to time, but we also know how weak we are with line editing or developmental editing. When we tell ourselves the truth, we know that if we release a manuscript that we edited ourselves, that it will be full of typos and grammatical glitches, and that the prose may not be the most clearly written expression of best narrative practice. We might be telling a great story, and our creative writing skills might be shining through, but the manuscript might look like a tenth grader typed it up.

Editors can be creative and original and innovative, but you never hire them to rewrite your writing. They are not collaborators in that sense. Their job is to interpret and clarify your intention as an author. This takes a particular talent and skill set, different than the skill set and talent of the author function. An editor's insightfulness and intuition about what an author is trying to say, as they try to parse dense and convoluted prose, are the key talents you are looking for in a developmental editor that is evaluating your manuscript. As a writer you might tie yourself into word-knots, mistakenly thinking you are crystal clear, but a good editor will show you how to untie those knots to better effect, often saving entire books in the process.

THE NATURE OF CONSULTANCY

The consultancy relationship is a two-way street. Both parties have responsibilities. For any relationship to work the partners need to be actively engaged, have trust, and hold one another in mutual respect. If these three things are not present, then you run the risk of either being run over by the consultant or becoming a traffic hazard, stopping the consultant from delivering what's promised.

It all begins with engagement, and you, the writer, are the initiator. Without you setting the right tone, expectation, and objective, the trust and respect will not be there, and the experience will probably be unpleasant (and costly). If you own a business or a home, then you already have some practical experience hiring vendors. When you hire a plumber to fix your pipes, you do your due diligence, right? You call around, get referrals, check reviews online, ask hard questions, make sure they're bonded and have the necessary experience. You set the tone (I'm the boss), have clear expectations (scope of work), and have a clear objective (deliverables). It should be no different with a script consultant or book editor.

I break them into two sets of five questions each: one set for the consultant, the other set for you. The idea here is that you have to get the consultant to jump through some hoops in order to vet them adequately so that you feel there is a basis for a reciprocal relationship but to also vet yourself (so to speak) to make sure you are prepared to undertake this effort. You don't want to waste their time or yours, so these questions are a great way to begin your process of hiring, or not, the consultant of your dreams.

Many business gurus have written on the best practices for interviewing third-party consultants. Consequently, there are many resources online to help you with standardized questions any consultant would expect in an interview: "What was your biggest success?" "What was your biggest failure?" How would you describe your greatest weakness and strength?" These are perfectly useful and utilitarian, but they are also expected and tend to generate canned responses. By all means, find these resources and use them; modify them or do whatever you have to do to customize them to your objectives.

What follows are ten questions specifically designed with you the writer in mind and geared for the specific application of the writing or story development engagement. Asking these questions will help set the tone, expectations, and results of the consulting engagement so that everyone's needs are met satisfactorily, or at least so that you don't get screwed.

FIVE QUESTIONS TO ASK THE CONSULTANT

#1: WHAT WAS YOUR PROFESSIONAL EXPERIENCE BEFORE YOU BECAME A CONSULTANT?"

M ost consultants have some facsimile of their work history on their websites under a "Clients" tab or as testimonials, but you want to know more than just their client list (we'll talk more about this later). What did they do before they were consulting? You're not interested in finding out if they had a paper route when they were ten, no. This is about what work they did in the field before they went solo. Questions like: Did they work in the field prior to becoming a consultant? What production companies, studios, or publishing houses did they work for? How long? What writers or projects of note did they work on when they were working in the field?

You might ask for a resume or curriculum vitae, but script consultants do not typically use these. If they don't have any prior industry experience (entertainment or publishing), that is a red flag that they may not have the depth and/or experience you need. In addition to the generic resume-like questions, there is value in finding out the following:

Do they have genre expertise?

If so, which ones. For book editors, how knowledgeable are they with *The Chicago Manual of Style*—any real editor will know this style guide well. There is no style guide for script consultants, not like in the book business, so it is hard to pretest their skill in this area. Here's where the resume plays heavily. If the screenwriter has worked for established companies, then it's pretty safe to assume they know their genres and formatting conventions. If they don't have any real professional experience with established production companies or producers, that is a red flag; not necessarily a show stopper, but a warning sign.

Do they present at industry events?

Ask editors if they present at writer conferences, festivals, and book fairs; if so, which ones? This is important to gauge if they are well established and respected in the literary community. The same question should be put to script consultants. It's not necessary they do these kinds of events, but it is a good sign if they do—it usually means they are well established and respected in their field.

What formats do they favor?

For script consultants that means hour drama, sitcom, feature film, animation, etc., for book editors that means short fiction, long fiction, nonfiction, series, comics, graphic novels, etc.

#2: HOW ARE YOUR CLIENTS BETTER OFF FOR WORKING WITH YOU, AND CAN I TALK TO SOME OF THEM?

If an editor or script consultant just gives you generic or spin-doctored answers to this, then you know they don't have a clue what their value is. By generic, I mean answers like: "My clients get a solid script at the end of the day," or "My clients end up with a good story they can sell and market," or "My clients ended up happy and positioned for success." These are all useless. You want to hear things like: "My clients walk away with a process they can use on their own that will help them succeed on their own," or "My clients are given specific marketing strategies they can use going forward for any book or script they write," or "My clients walk away with a professional level of understanding of story development and story struc-ture." These can be spin doctoring too, and sales talk, but at least they show the editor or consultant has clear deliverables and a process in place (more on this later).

Checking References

Then ask to talk to former clients. They may just have a few friends lined up to spin for them; you can't ever know, but hopefully not. Regardless, ask to talk to former clients, at least two. If the editor or consultant balks because of confidentiality issues, this might be valid if they have a confidentiality agreement in place but ask anyway. How they react to this question can tell you a lot about their integrity and their willingness to be transparent. It's a red flag if they get defensive or deflect with legalities and other objections. Vetting your consultant's references is essential. It's the only way you can be sure you're dealing with someone who has a proven professional record versus someone who is just a great performer in an interview.

Chances are you won't get a complete list of references, but rather a partial list of cherry-picked clients. That's fine. Take what they give you but ask for the whole list to see if they respond. It is often valuable to ask the consultant to highlight any clients on the list they do give you who dealt with the same or similar problems that you might be facing. In each case, call the person who supervised the consultant's work directly and start your talk with an open-ended question, "I'm thinking about hiring Joe to edit my book. I understand you hired him for the same purpose. How did that work out?"

Today, many people will not comment about the performance of former consultants for fear of lawsuits if they give a negative recommendation that results in loss of work for the consultant. So, if you can't get them to open up freely, just focus on the basics: the kind of problems the consultant addressed, services provided, and the duration of the work. Then sneak in some questions to get more personal insight, like, "Would you hire this person again?" or "Would you recommend this consultant to a friend?"

Whether the reference is forthcoming or not, you should pay attention to what's not being said. If the reference only talks about the consultant's great work ethic, good attitude, and fantastic communication skills, be sure to ask if his or her work met the objectives and expectations for which they were hired. Also, ask if the job was completed at the negotiated price—or if it went over budget with financial and project scope creep.

Finally, you should end with another open-ended question that gives the reference one last chance to expand on their previous comments. "What else can you tell me about Joe?" or, "If you had it to do over again, are there any areas of the project, or of working with Joe, that you would do differently today?"

#3: DO YOU HAVE A METHODOLOGY OR PROCESS YOU USE WITH EVERY CLIENT, OR DO YOU JUST "GO WITH THE FLOW"?

So many writers hire an editor or consultant, hand over their book or script, then walk away, waiting for the final results to be handed to them. Big mistake. You have to find out how the editor or consultant works. What is their workflow? How do they handle their financial flow? Do they have a refund policy? How will they deliver feedback?

Does the editor or consultant have sample manuscripts, notes, or coverage they can give you, so that you can see their approach? Does the book editor use Microsoft Word "track changes" to document all edits and comments inline in the manuscript (this is essential), or do they wing it in a text file with a bunch of colored test inserts (crazy-making)?

Professionals, regardless of their industry, have established process procedures and deliverables for every client. You have a right to know those process procedures and the nature of the final product before they start work. This is critical because the way the editor or consultant answers this question tells you boat loads about their professionalism, experience, and attitude toward you, the client. Ignoring this question can set you up for scope creep, battles over poor work and redoes, and a host of other consulting nightmares.

#4: WILL YOU DO A SAMPLE EDIT?

It is not at all uncommon for book editors to give a free editing sample of your manuscript (usually no more than a few pages), so that you can see their process. Script consultants typically do not do this, which I think is a bad policy. Sometimes script consultants will give a free mini-consult over the phone and talk about your script and give some feedback, and perhaps this can suffice as a "sample," but most script consultants won't work on the actual script without being hired first. In this case, it's reasonable for you as the client to ask for a mini-evaluation, or consult, to get some sense of the consultant's ability to quickly assess your story or writing.

If they refuse, this is not a sign (necessarily) that they are jerks, but it is reasonable to ask them why they won't do it? Maybe they have a good answer, perhaps not. Just asking can tell you a lot about how they are approaching the relationship. Book editors will usually not hesitate to give a free sample edit, but some may. Use your judgment and always ask "why not," if for no other reason than to get a sense of how they'll respond, and then make your decisions accordingly.

#5: WILL YOU SIGN A CONTRACT?

Contracts exist for one reason: the two parties hate each other, won't talk things through, and refuse to compromise—thank goodness for contracts. Even so, this is problematic for a lot of people, because they don't want the hassle of making contracts, maybe hiring a lawyer, negotiating, etc. And for small, one-off projects, contracts can feel like overkill (and they are). But, there is a tangible and intangible reason for asking the question.

The intangible reason is that you want to see how they'll react. If they are firm and tell you they never make contracts (script consultants almost never do), and they feel solid and clean (no agendas) about it, then you'll probably be okay, but you should still insist on putting something short and specific in writing. If they say "no, I don't do those," and it feels avoidant and defensive, then you're probably on shaky ground. And if they say "no, I don't do those, but what would work for you?" then you are okay. Working without some form of an agreement opens you to misery if there is a dispute.

The tangible reason for a contract is when you have a long or complicated project with due dates, deliverables, and many moving parts. Like I said, script consultants almost never make contracts and will surely push back, so it's just a psychological game you're playing when you ask the question. But book editors are more accustomed to contracts. Most professional editors operate under the best practices set up by the Editorial Freelancers Association (EFA)* and use contract templates and pricing schedules based on the *EFA's recommendations. Long or involved projects need contracts, especially those stretching into the thousands of dollars in consulting fees.

Contracts are too complicated to discuss here, but they are not rocket science, and there are good samples online you can use to guide you. Once you create one, you just clone it for future jobs. I cannot stress enough the importance of having your professional working relationship spelled out with third-party vendors before you engage them to work. It's your time and money, so gamble accordingly.

*Note: Editorial Freelancers Association's rate card is available online, but it is not always the most current source of rates for freelancers as it tends to lag behind actual market fees. It is also on the low end of most scales for experienced freelancers. But, it *is a great resource and a good place to start negotiations. Always do your research and find as many resources as possible to calculate realistic market rates. Researching top editorial superstar consultants, and their website rates is a good place to start along with the EFA.*

FIVE QUESTIONS TO ASK YOURSELF

As stated earlier, you have a crucial role to play in the consultancy relationship. Most business how-to advice about hiring third-parties only focuses on how to hire someone else, and rarely, if ever, turns the examination back on the interviewer. Are you ready to hire a consultant? Are you prepared to be a boss? Are you in a place where you need a consultant? There are many questions you need to be truthful with yourself about, but that you may not even know you should be asking. Below are five basic questions that can help you do a quick self-assessment to see if you are situated to engage in a third-party hire properly.

#1: CAN YOU AFFORD THEM?

Pricing is always a tricky topic when hiring a third-party. Usually, consultants will have their fee schedules posted on their websites, so you know going in what to expect. With script consultants there are no best practices for charging fees; it's pretty much "make it up as you go along." Things that can affect pricing might be their years in the business, big client lists, professional credits, etc. The bottom line here is you will have to gauge for yourself if you think their fees are agreeable or not. But, how can you know?

Are there any standards you can use to compare and contrast? Or are you just stuck going with their first quote and ending up with "you get what you pay for"? The smartest approach is to do your research; check out as many other consultants as you can and compare pricing and services. You will quickly get a feel for the market, and then you can determine if that outrageous fee they're asking for is value-added and justified or not. Script consulting pricing is the wild west, and there's not much you can do about it, so do your homework and then draw your lines in the sand based on your budget and your research.

Everything I just said about script consultants also applies to book editors, except that there are some best practices in place for freelance book editor's fees. As mentioned earlier, the Editorial Freelancers Association (EFA) has posted standard rates for all categories of editorial work. These are just starting points for negotiating a deal, but at least you can know what is considered fair and right within the profession. So, buyer beware, do your homework.

#2: ARE YOU COMFORTABLE WITH THE CONSULTANT'S CLIENTS' PUBLISHING/PRODUCING RECORDS?

When you hire an editor or script consultant you are hiring an editor first and a writer second. I say this because people incorrectly ascribe competence as an editor or story consultant based on how many books they've written or screenplays they've sold. This is irrelevant. Editorial talent is different than writing talent.

Beginning writers are not the only ones who make this mistake. Consider this: "I think it would be nice if the guy writing the book on how to write a screenplay had actually sold something! Don't you think? (Blake Snyder. *Save the Cat*, Michael Wiese Productions 2005, pp xii).

Blake Snyder was one of the great screenwriting story gurus, and still, he fell for this misconception hook line and sinker. Becoming produced or published indicates that you have written something someone else wants to buy. They see commercial potential. They see profit. They see a way to advance their agenda through your good works as a writer. Not bad, not wrong—just the business of writing. Does it necessarily follow from a sale that you are a good writer? Does it necessarily follow that you are an expert in story structure or storytelling? Does selling your book or screenplay mean you know more about writing than someone who hasn't sold something? The answer to all those questions is a loud and in-your-face no. Lots of bad writers sell things, lots of writers who sell things know little or nothing about storytelling (they may be good writers, but lousy storytellers—writing and storytelling are two different things) and lots of writers who have sold something can't teach their way out of a paper bag. Selling does not equate to competent or qualified. Selling only means you write well enough to attract buyers (no small thing, I grant you).

There is no question that writers who have sold their work know more about the experience and business of being a working writer than writers who have not gone through that experience. They also may have some deeper appreciation of the writing process and some original ideas about how to write. But, selling isn't the key. Experience is the key. Writers who have been through the publishing and movie production mills have a rich experience that they should share with anyone who will listen. There is real value there. But, if they haven't sold anything, that doesn't mean they have less experience or insight.

That doesn't disqualify them from being wise teachers with something important to say (if they have anything to say at all— not all do). That doesn't relegate them to some lesser status. It only means they haven't hit the lottery. Because that's what selling a script or book is more akin to than anything else. It's consistency, persistence, and a refusal to take "no" for an answer that gets you produced or published. It will happen eventually. But, even if it takes decades, that is not a statement that your qualifications are lacking, it is a statement about the business problem of selling your widget. Being produced or published is a business problem, not a writing problem because it isn't enough to have a good story. Lots of "good stories" end up in the round file and will never get seen or read. So, I repeat with emphasis: getting produced or published is a business problem, not a writing problem.

But, I suspect that what I'm saying will not convince many people. So, let me give you a historical example. Let me tell you a little story—the story of Maxwell Perkins.

From 1910 until the early 1950s, Max was a developmental editor at Charles Scribner's Sons, one of the top publishing companies in the world. Even today, he is regarded as the greatest editor of all time. His authors included: Ernest Hemingway, F. Scott Fitzgerald, Thomas Wolf, Ring Lardner, Marjorie Rawlings, Alan Paton, Thomas Mann—you get the idea. Perkins was single-handedly responsible for saving the careers of Ring Lardner and Thomas Wolf and for getting two Nobel Prizes in Literature for two of his other authors, Hemingway and Fitzgerald.

Perkins was a master storyteller, not a writer. He knew story better than anyone in his generation. The results of his authors proved his skill and talent. So, do you think Hemingway asked him, "Hey Max, before I let you work on *The Sun Also Rises*, tell me, how many novels have your written? I don't think you should be giving me advice unless you've been published yourself."

Uh—no. Hemingway never asked that. Nor did Fitzgerald, or Wolf or the other dozen famous writers who begged Perkins for his help. Maxwell Perkins never published so much as a recipe his entire professional career. According to the wisdom of our current crop of story consultant naysayers, Perkins would be considered a snake oil salesman, a guy who consults rather than does, a wannabe, etc.

Perkins was an editor, a developmental editor. He had a skill that most writers don't have: the ability to structure and develop a narrative that leverages the writing talents of the author. This is a specific and complex skill set. It is a skill set that does not require the ability to sell a book or screenplay, and it does not require being published or produced. Being a good editor is a talent, one that can make or break careers and multi-million-dollar projects.

Screenwriting consultants (or book consultants) are no different than Maxwell Perkins (okay, maybe not so talented). They are doing the same kind of work; they are essentially developmental editors. I don't care if it's for a production company, studio, movie star, or a publisher. The function is the same: consultants leverage a screenwriter's talents and show the writer how to tell the story to its best advantage.

This is a skill set most screenwriters don't have. Authors may write well, but they may not know how to tell a story properly. I know this to be the case because I see it all the time with my published and produced clients (remember—writing and story-telling are two different skills and have nothing to do with one another!).

Consequently, if you are going to measure the worth of any consultant, then the measure should not be in the man or woman's sales record, but in the successes and-or failures of their client list. How many books or screenplays have their clients sold? How many bestsellers, writing competition wins, or awards have their writers won? When you hire a consultant the only track records that matter are the track records of all the other writers who have come before you that have hired and relied on that consultant's advice. Client successes are the only metrics that count.

So, ask book editors what publishing successes their clients have had; ask script consultant how many of their clients got script sales, awards, or producing deals. You will have to weigh how comfortable you are hiring an "expert" with a client list filled with low-sale, self-published books with terrible Amazon category rankings; or a script consultant with few or no clients with produced IMDB (Internet Movie Database) credits or festival awards. Again, having a weak client list doesn't mean they can't do the job, but know going in so you can be fully informed in your decision-making process.

When you hire an editor or script consultant you are hiring an editor first and a writer second. I say this because people incorrectly ascribe competence as an editor or story consultant based on how many books they've written or screenplays they've sold. This is irrelevant. Editorial talent is different than writing talent.

#3: ARE YOU WILLING TO FIRE THE CONSULTANT IF YOU ARE DISSATISFIED WITH THE WORK OR THE RELATIONSHIP?

Are you comfortable managing them, and not being managed by them? Because if you don't take control of the relationship, the consultant will—by necessity. The consulting relationship will go off the rails unless someone is managing the process. That "someone" should be the client, not the consultant. Part of that process involves hiring but also firing. Can you do that? It's easier said than done for a lot of people. Most people want to avoid conflict and will ride out the experience and move on, losing money, time, and their sanity. But it doesn't have to be that way.

Build checkpoints into the relationship so that you can measure progress and discuss problems, delays, or failure sooner than later. In short one-off projects, this is less of an issue, but you still have to be willing to step up and fire the consultant if things are going south and you are not happy. This is where contracts are important. Termination clauses need to be written so that you can fire someone cleanly and with as little exposure as possible on your end. If you don't get a contract, at least get written agreement in an email explaining your criteria for releasing the consultant if you are unhappy. The bottom line here is: Are you willing to be a boss and not a passive player in some consultant's agenda?

#4: CAN THEY DO AN INTERVIEW AND WALK AND CHEW GUM AT THE SAME TIME?

It should be obvious that asking the first five questions will require talking to the editor or consultant. If at all possible, talk to them over the phone or video chat. Don't settle for texting or email. How they present in person can tell you a lot about how comfortable they are with you and vice versa. Can they talk clearly? Do they make sense? Are they confident? Do they ask you questions and not just passively wait for you to ask them? Do they leave you feeling they can do the job and that they like what they're doing? That's more of an issue than you might imagine.

~

#5: WHAT KIND OF CONSULTANT DO YOU REALLY NEED?

All consultants and editors are not created equal. Many consultants will tell you they do it all; don't believe them. It's best to work with professionals who specialize in one type of editing, not doubling or tripling up on skill sets. Here are the basic types of editors and consultants you will need:

Line Editors

These are the "small picture" editors focusing on grammar, punctuation, sentence structure, consistency of word usage, spelling, and some rewriting, but at a very light level. They should have a solid understanding and knowledge of *The Chicago Manual of Style*—this is the main style guide used in the book business. Their job is one of crossing t's and dotting i's (novels, nonfiction, newspaper/magazine copy, online content). Copy-editing is essentially the same thing as line editing.

Proof Readers

A proofreader is the last person to get their eyes on the manuscript. They essentially "proof" the final typeset text, the final approval before it goes to actual press. Outside the special world of the publishing company, proofers are often just seen as another kind of line editor, but they are more than that. Even after line editing, you may want to hire a proofreader to do the final-final on your manuscript, but that all depends on the competency level of your line editor.

Developmental Editors

These are the "big picture" editors. They focus on storytelling, author voice, narrative design, research, book formatting and organization, make suggestions on story or content revisions, and generally assure the manuscript is well-organized, consistent in style and tone, and clearly articulated as a piece of fiction or nonfiction. Sometimes they'll fact check, but this is usually a separate person.

TYPES OF SCREENWRITING CONSULTANTS

Story/Development Consultants

These consultants are essentially developmental editors but

specialize in the film/TV format. Story consultants focus on the big picture, just as book editors do, and concern themselves with the large story structure, pacing, formatting, and narrative flow issues that any developmental editor would be concerned with in a fiction or nonfiction narrative. The key difference between them and book developmental editors is that they have expertise in feature film, television, and new media storytelling vs long-form prose fiction/nonfiction.

Pitching Consultants

Pitching consultants specialize in preparing you to pitch your film or television projects to contests, pitchfests, or to production companies. They help you come up with a great logline, develop a "pitch package/deck," identify market opportunities, write a good synopsis, and may have some other value-added services to set themselves apart in the marketplace.

Story Analysts

These consultants are the workhorses of the script evaluation business. Commonly known as "readers," story analysts provide industry standard coverage, which is a standard deliverable common to creative agencies, production companies, studios, and indie producers. Readers are usually not something indie writers would have to worry about unless their script got picked up by an interested agency or producer; however, many script evaluation services have emerged offering this service.

Adaptation Consultants

These consultants help you adapt your screenplay to the novel format or the other way around. They will help you rewrite your book or screenplay, depending on which service you seek, and guide the process so the final deliverable will be a marketable book or screenplay. This requires specialized understanding of either the publishing and prose worlds, or the film/TV worlds, so it is essential to make sure the consultant has experience in their given area.

The more you are exposed to professionals, the smarter you will become in recognizing those who are genuinely talented and productive. You will have to kill a lot of frogs, however, before you find your prince.

CONCLUSION

Asking these ten questions will help you not only find the right editor or script consultant but will make you the kind of client consultants will enjoy working with. The snake-oil-salesmen hucksters will quickly expose themselves, and the gems in the rough will always shine through. Writing is a lonely game, but you don't have to do all of it alone—in fact, you can't—if you expect a real career. Learn the skills for hiring third-parties and empower yourself with the confidence and composure that comes from knowing what you want, and not giving your power away to any expert or consultant.

THE END

EPILOGUE

WHAT IT MEANS TO BE A CONSCIOUS WRITER

This series of books covers many diverse topics, but one topic that spans across the entire series, touching every book, is the subject of "the conscious writer." Consequently, even if the book you are reading does not mention this concept explicitly, it is implicitly embedded in every paragraph, in every bullet point, and in every topic heading.

The idea of the conscious writer is so fundamental to my teaching and consulting that it has become not just a motto, but a manifesto. It's something I would chip into sidewalks or spray-paint on blank walls under freeway overpasses, and on abandoned buildings, if I could (without risking fines or jail time).

The origin of this idea came out of my evolution as a writer, but even more so it came from watching the thousands of consulting clients I've had over the years, both prose writers and screen-writers. Seeing how many of them were sleepwalking through their writing careers, blindly following how-to, creative writing memes, or obediently applying pointless paradigms and theories to their writing forced me to not only wake up in my own writing process, but to realize that "everyone deserved to be woken from their writing somnambulism and deserved to at least be given the opportunity to take back their creative power from whatever guru, methodology, or flavor-of-the-month, creative-writing secret sauce they may have given their power away to. Yes, I'm talking about empowerment.

The word "empowerment" is way overused these days, having been effectively highjacked by the self-help and human poten-tial movements of the 1980s and 1990s. But empowerment means something, and it means something important for creative people in particular. It means: giving yourself the permission and giving yourself the authority (authorship) to be powerful. Being powerful means: having the ability and the willingness to act. When you are empowered you are giving yourself permission to have power (i.e., exercise your ability and willingness to act). You cannot be powerful or empowered without being awake and conscious. The trances of the gurus are broken, and the charms of the writing-process charismatics are dispelled. It's time that writers took back the word "empow-erment" and made it our own.

We live in an age where it has become frighteningly easy to go on autopilot and hand over creative control to "experts, gurus, teachers, or some authority. Being a conscious writer is all about taking your creative power back and taking full responsibility for "your writing process, creativity, writing successes, and writing failures. So, to that end, I have created the "Seven Qualities of the Conscious Writer." Read them, live them, breath them not as some new dogma handed down from some new writing guru, but as wisdom you can choose or reject as you wish. Take what works, reject what doesn't; then, move on—by choice!

THE SEVEN QUALITIES OF A CONSCIOUS WRITER:

- They intentionally make narrative choices based on creative objectives and goals; they do not stumble in the story dark, tripping into a story clueless how they got there.
- They know what they are writing, why they are writing it, and how they want to write it.
- They are always open to new approaches to storytelling and creative writing, and never dogmatic about any one approach.
- They are so steeped in the fundamentals of story development, and the best practices of creative writing that whenever they choose to stray from those fundamentals and best practices they do so with sure

footedness, creative poise, and confidence in their craft.

- They listen to everyone, try everything, but follow no one; they are their own guru.
- They take responsibility for their failures as well as their successes and know that they (not some fortune cookie) are the only ones who can solve their writing problems—and they love that responsibility.
- They don't give their creative power away to anyone or anything—ever.

Being a conscious writer honors our true creative process and is the only path to achieve deep, authentic, and meaningful connection with readers. It is the best way to be your best writer-self.

REMEMBER: LISTEN TO EVERYONE, TRY EVERYTHING, FOLLOW NO ONE. YOU ARE YOUR OWN STORY GURU."

PART IV

RAPID STORY DEVELOPMENT #4: TEAMS AND ENSEMBLES—HOW TO DEVELOP STORIES WITH LARGE CASTS

STORY FUNCTION VS. STORY FORM

I don't think there is a single creative person in the world who has not heard the phrase "form follows function." It was the famous mentor of the American architect Frank Lloyd Wright, Louis H. Sullivan, who first expressed the notion that form follows function, in an artistic context, in his 1896 article "The Tall Office Building Artistically Considered":

"It is the pervading law of all things organic and inorganic, of all things physical and metaphysical, of all things human and all things superhuman, of all true manifestations of the head, of the heart, of the soul, that the life is recognizable in its expression, that form ever follows function. This is the law." [1]

Just as a chair (form) expresses the purpose of "sitting" (function), just as a house (form) expresses the feeling of "home" (function), and just as an open space (form) expresses the experience of "freedom," so a story (form) expresses the act of story-telling (function).

Form and function in creative writing are different things, but they are self-supporting, meaning: they each make the other more effective. You cannot tell a story without it taking some shape, be that shape a dance, or painting, or mime act, or sculpture, or song, or even the written word. The literary forms that stories take, i.e., the physical expression of storytelling in the world of literature, have a technical name: genre.

Genres are story forms, i.e., agreed upon conventions of artistic composition and stylistic expression. Storytelling is story function, i.e., the natural purpose or final intention of a story. Genre and storytelling exist in a balanced and cooperative state such that storytelling is made more powerful and effective by genre in transferring the experience of being human from person to person. That is the central purpose (function) of storytelling; it is how we teach one another about what it means to be human. Story forms are purely in service to the function of telling a story.

Genre forms can exist on their own, but in the absence of a story to tell genres tend to become empty shells and typically deliver lackluster and dead experiences for readers or viewing audiences. A genre without a story is like romance without love. As a reader or movie lover, you have experienced this. Who hasn't read that mediocre novel, or watched that dull movie and walked away feeling like the experience was one dimension, dramatically flat, and unoriginal? Okay, maybe there were lots of zombies, and car chases; or aliens, robots, and superheroes, but—been there, done that. Without a story, genre loses its significance. When something loses its significance, it loses its ability to impact or change us. Thus, in the "right hands," genres can elevate, inspire, augment, deepen, and generally make better any story to which it is in service. In the "wrong hands," genre may entertain and distract, but it will never find the higher calling that comes from telling a story. This is not bad or wrong, but it is not storytelling.

SO WHAT? CAN'T I JUST HAVE FUN?

Of course, you can. In fact, I would hope that you have fun with everything you write. But, not every author sets out to change the world, sometimes they write just for the fun of it. But, herein lies the reason for this discussion. When you write, do you set out with an intention from the start? Other than to finish, what is your plan? Do you have one? Do you have any clue about what it is you are saying? And if you have nothing to say, then what is the objective?

We are taught in the consensus school of creative writing that you should just "go for it." Writers write, so you don't have to have a plan. You don't have to know what your message is (if you have one). You just have to put your butt in a chair and do it. Good stories write themselves. Good characters write themselves. Don't think about it; just write.

For 99.9 per cent of writers, this is the worst writing advice they will ever receive. It is the number one creative writing myth that you must bust if you are to become a better writer (see my e-book, *Rapid Story Development #2: How to Bust the Top Ten Creative Writing Myths to Become a Better Writer*). But within this myth is a gem of an idea: How conscious do you want to be when it comes to knowing what kind of writer you are? How aware are you when you apply the various story and writing tools you have in your creative toolbox to the stories you want to tell?

In "Appendix 2" I discuss in some detail the concept of being a conscious writer; an idea I find to be essential in the development of not just writers, but any creative artist. But it begs the question: Are you out to entertain and give the reader a wild ride, or are you out to do both of those things and tell a story that might teach your reader a little bit about what it means to be human?

If your answer is the latter, then this e-book is essential to your growth as a conscious writer. To accomplish all the tasks you have before you (entertain, inform, inspire, and teach a reader), you must master the crafts of story form and story function. You have to know the purpose of your writing (function) and then consciously choose the best expression (genre/form) to achieve your purpose, and they are two separate craft skills, so they must be learned separately.

Before we continue and get into the substance of this e-book, and the nature of team and ensemble stories, it is essential to understand a little about what genres are, why they are important, and the role they play in storytelling in order to appreciate the place that team and ensemble stories occupy in the grand scheme of story expression.

WHAT IS A GENRE AND WHY SHOULD I CARE?

As readers, we are all exposed to genre forms with every book we read: mystery, detective, horror, romance, etc. Every book, movie, short story, in fact, any form of storytelling belongs to a genre. This is a bit of a controversial statement, but I believe it to be true. From the highest-concept, zombie-apocalypse, young-adult-dystopian actioner to the most introspective, internal-angsty, navel-contemplating "literary" novel all stories fall into some genre form.

Who says? And who has been put in charge of defining these so-called forms and validating that they meet the necessary requirements to be a genre? The answer will surprise you. The "who" is not some lofty literary critic in a big New York publishing company, or a rarified literary society tucked away in some dusty, book-lined mausoleum. No, the "who" is you (and me).

Readers are the ones who create genres. How? By their reading habits, buying patterns, and writer loyalties. We like what we like. And when an author gives us what we like, we ask for more of the same. But we don't want just a rehash of what we read before, we want something new, but—the same. Our demand of the writer is clear, "Give us the same pace, the same big story beats, similar structure components, but make each story original and surprising. If you do that, I'll keep coming back for more."

That's the deal; the arrangement, unspoken as it may be,

between authors and readers. This is how genres are born—and die. Readers tell authors, not how to write, but the parameters of what they want to read. Out of this reader-writer dance, all the genres we know have come into existence. And, because of this arrangement, we continue to see new genres emerge in the market on a regular basis, as well as old genres that fall from grace.

Just in the last several years, the "Young Adult (YA)" genre (12–18) has spawned a new genre: "New Adult" fiction (*The Simple Wild* by K.A. Tucker, *Bring Down the Stars* by Emma Scott). Older readers (18–30) who enjoyed YA stories kept asking for YA-like adventures but with more mature characters dealing with more adult issues, and New Adult was born. Similarly, as climate change has become a major issue in the world, so litera-ture has reflected its importance. The new genre "Climate Fiction (Cli-Fi)" has emerged to respond to reader interest in climate-oriented stories (*American War* by Omar El-Akkad, *The Year of the Flood* by Margaret Atwood).

TEAM & ENSEMBLE FORMS

Within all the familiar genres we know and love, there are two subforms that are of interest to us in this e-book: team stories and ensemble stories. They are not genres, per se, but they operate in a genre-like fashion. You would no more write a horror story the same way you would a romance than you would write a team story the same way you would write an ensemble story. Both forms have their own qualities, story beats, pacing, and unique elements that distinguish one from the other.

Many writers have heard about ensemble stories, but the idea of a team story is not so familiar. When I suggest to writers that teams are an essential part of character building in some stories, I am usually met with blank stares and confused looks. The idea that teams or team-building concepts might have anything to do with storytelling rarely if ever, occurs to people. On the surface of things, the natural connection between teams and fiction is not an intuitive one, but when the concept—as a story development tool— is explained logically, most people warm to the concept and see the sense of it—but getting there takes some theoretical bridge building and some practical demonstration.

The theoretical piece requires understanding one basic distinction: the difference between an ensemble and a team. As for the practical demonstration, that can be accomplished by showing how teams operate within specific genres to support not just individual character development, but the overall development of a story's structure.

To that end, what follows in this e-book is a systematic breakdown of each of these two subforms of story expression, followed by examples of each, and detailed nuances that must be mastered when writing any team or ensemble format.

First, we will examine the "pure" forms of each, meaning we will look at the theory and practical examples of teams and ensembles where they do not overlap or get muddled with cross-pollination, as genres are want to do. Then, after we look at the pure forms, we will examine the "gray zone," where teams and ensembles can overlap and mix, potentially confusing the presentation, but often still ending up with effective and entertaining results.

As with all things story, there are few black and white scenarios on how to do anything. Genres all mix together, story forms all blend together, and there's no one way to do anything, but there are best practices. These are what you need to learn, not in some slavish way, but in the spirit of Pablo Picasso's famous quote, "Learn the rules like a pro, so you can break them like an artist."

----

[1] Sullivan, Louis H. (1896). "The Tall Office Building Artistically Considered". Lippincott's Magazine (March 1896): 403–409

THE TEAM STORY

W e begin with a simple question and definition: what is a team?

> *"A group of people with a full set of complementary skills required to complete a task, job, or project. Team members (1) operate with a high degree of interdependence, (2) share authority and responsibility for self-management, (3) are accountable for the collective performance, and (4) work toward a common goal and shared rewards(s)."* [1]

This definition is a bit dry and not all that useful for creative writing, but it does capture the essence of what a team is and the qualities needed to constitute a team. The only other element that might be added is one of time. A team is most often constituted around a common goal to be achieved over a certain period of time. Teams that have long-term missions can still be seen as teams, i.e., the Human Resources Department can be a team, or the Shipping Department can be a team, but they are not assembled to do a discreet task in a defined period of time, like say a writers room on a television show.

As writers, we are more concerned with this time-sensitive application of the team concept. Teams in fictional stories need to have a time-limited mission, but not operate across unmanageable time scales. How long is too long? How short a timescale is necessary? This is subjective and individual to each story and group of characters, but when you start pushing things into years, you may be weakening the function of the team concept. Most often we're talking hours, days, weeks, or months. It all depends on if you can maintain the feel of a team under pressure, while you cast the time net for the story out across an expansive or unforeseeable end. Perhaps you can already see some of the challenges that start presenting themselves when you begin to think in terms of teams, and not just in terms of a cast of characters.

TEAMS VS GROUPS

It is essential to make a distinction early in our discussion between a team and a group (or working group). Groups are collectives of individuals all of whom have something in common, or who share information that can help individuals achieve individual goals or tasks. Groups do not have the internal cohesion of teams, nor do they have the characteristics of teams in fictional stories (see later chart).

Groups, as such, tend to have much more in common with ensembles than teams. Because they share some common interest or knowledge, they can appear more interdependent and team-like than they are. As we will see later, this is often one of the key factors that confuse readers and viewers when they come upon a story that is an ensemble story but possesses group characteristics that muddy the dramatic waters. In the last chapter, we will look at some examples of this phenomenon, which will illustrate how nothing in creative writing is just black or white; but black, white, and shades of gray.

TEAM DEFINITION FOR WRITERS

While the team definition offered at the beginning of this chapter is technically accurate for defining a team in business, it is not perhaps the best definition for creative writers. So, let me present an alternative definition of a team story that you can use in developing your own team stories.

A team in fictional stories is defined as:

1. A set of two or more people with a full or partial selection of complimentary skills,

- or non-complementary skills (that later become complimentary),
- required to achieve a common goal,
- that ultimately serves to accomplish the telling of a story.

2. Team members:

- operate on a sliding scale of interdependence from low to high as the team develops, ultimately becoming highly interdependent,
- share responsibility for team evolution and efficacy,
- are accountable for team successes and failures,
- share collectively in performance-related rewards and punishments,
- work toward achieving a common goal(s) or outcome(s).

The chief differences between this definition and the earlier definition are that this definition recognizes the variability in team size, but especially notes how small a team can be. It also points to that common skill sets required by team members may not necessarily be complimentary. Indeed, in many team stories, members of the team may have uncomplimentary skills that only later after team cohesion occurs, prove to be complimentary. An example of this is when a new team member comes onboard and does not seem to have any skills whatsoever, until later in the story circumstances arise that prove this person has an essential skill the team did not value or recognize initially.

THE FOUR STAGES OF TEAM DEVELOPMENT

In addition to the new definition of a team offered above, there is another defining quality of a team story that is always overlooked by writers: *stages of development.*

Just as individual human beings have interpersonal dynamics, so teams have internal dynamics that make them run, fall apart, or perform at peak efficiency. Teams don't just happen, they coalesce over time, and they all follow a similar developmental process. All teams in the real world go through four stages of development:

THE STAGES

• Forming[2]: The team orients itself in three areas: goals or tasks, membership, and leadership.

• Storming: Conflict arises between the team and leader, and/or between individual team members.

• Norming: The team develops consensual working agreements over previous disagreements, or over new suggestions for team effectiveness.

• Performing: The team becomes extremely productive and effective; there is team synergy and high morale.

These same four stages apply to teams in the not-so-real world as well, i.e., the world of storytelling. Every book, film, or television show has teams operating in many different forms and in many different capacities.

People routinely throw around the word "team" when describing certain kinds of stories, because the team configuration is obvious. Most sports stories involve a literal team (*The Art of Fielding*, by Chad Harbach; *Hoosiers*, Orion Pictures; *Beartown*, by Fredrik Backman), action movies with military units fighting off the monster/alien/super-villain are obvious teams (*The Dirty Dozen*, Metro-Goldwyn-Mayer; *The Expendables*, Millennium Films; *A League of Their Own*, Columbia Pictures), or any group of people working together to do something is easily seen as team-like.

But, what about a love story? What about a one-man or one-woman show in the theater? What about a coming-of-age, teenage-angsty YA novel? As you will soon see, these all qualify as team stories (yes, even love stories). Remember the partial definition of a team: "*A group of people with a full set of complementary skills required to complete a task …*" The word "group" in this context doesn't just include a large cast of characters. "Group" can be just two or more people. But, even with a one-person show, there are other criteria (as you will see below) for a team story that apply that place such stories firmly into the team category.

The real defining piece that makes this approach to team stories unique and powerful is the idea of stages of development. This is game-changing information and will help you immensely in not only recognizing team stories when you see them but also writing them more effectively in your own fiction.

YEAH—BUT ...

One thing needs to be made clear at this point regarding team stages. While teams in real life always go through stages of development, teams in stories may not be so predictable. There are certain genres where team stories are more certain to have clearly defined stages than others. "Appendix 1" illustrates one such genre and gives a clear example of how stages play out. But some genres do not always cooperate in this clearcut way. Love stories, or quiet family dramas, or other genres will often suggest the presence of stages, but they may not be fully formed. If this is the case, it does not mean you do not have a team story. It means you have a team story with weakly defined stages. In other words, as with genre story beats, team stages of development will always be present in any team-based story.

For example, in most stories, there will always be a clear sense of the forming stage (characters come together), and there is usually a clear storming stage (characters start fighting over something), however short it may be, but the norming or performing stages may be weak or missing. The idea here is not to dismiss the team approach to writing because the stages might be lackluster in any particular story. The principles still apply and work. Maybe you can take the idea of stages and use it to strengthen the story, or maybe you need to realize that stages are not that important in this story, so you can let them go? The point is: you can't know which is best until you apply the ideas and the concepts of stages of development.

TEAM CHARACTERISTICS

Along with the four stages of team development, another feature that distinguishes team stories from ensembles is that team stories have specific characteristics distinct from ensembles in the structure of how a team story is told.

There are six basic characteristics that are almost always present in any team story:

Team Characteristics
A protagonist carries the story
The story is focused on a single main goal/task
The plot is time sensitive
Subplots are at service to the mainline story
Develops in stages that build dramatic cohesion
Story lines tend to be continuous, not episodic

As with stages, some of these characteristics may be missing or weakly drawn in a story, but generally speaking, they will all be present, especially the first two characteristics.

I don't want to spend a lot of time here detailing each characteristic here, as we will revisit each of these in a couple of chapters in more detail, but some of these do need a little explanation.

A protagonist carries the story.

There is a clear hero/heroine. The story is about someone in particular.

The story is focused on a single main goal/task.

The story will not be split when it comes to what the big objective of the story. There will be a goal, and it will be clear.

The plot is time sensitive.

In keeping with the definition of a team, the clock is usually ticking in a team story, not always, but usually.

Subplots are in service to the mainline story.

This is always a tough story development element in any story, regardless whether it is a team or ensemble story. But, in the best stories, subplots work best when they help to support the mainline story and do not act as competing, standalone stories within stories.

The story develops in stages.

As defined earlier, team stories have stages. Ensemble stories don't.

Stories tend to be continuous, not episodic.

Team stories follow a continuous narrative line of cause and effect. They do not follow episodic or sporadic styles of storytelling.

Once again, sometimes team stories can still manage to follow the team format despite having some of these characteristics weakly played or missing, but usually, they will all be present to one degree or another. If you see the first, second, and fifth characteristics present, those are enough to clearly identify the form as a team story.

TEAM ROLES

We have covered a new definition of "team" for writers, described four unique stages of development present in team stories, and presented specific characteristics common to all team stories. But, there is one other identifier that you can look for to help define and clarify the presence of a team story: team roles.

This is a complicated topic, and in some ways beyond the scope of this small e-book, but we need to discuss team roles at least at the high-level. For our purposes here, the central point I want to bring forward is the idea that in a team story all the team members have a role to play. In other words, there is no member of the team who is there because the author thinks it is just cool to have them there. Every team member has a story job to do, a developmental stage role to fulfill, and provides some window into the main character's personal situation. Let's take each of these separately:

Every member has a story job.

This may be obvious, but you would be surprised how quickly

the cast can get out of control if every character does not have a specific job to do in the functioning of the team and/or in the achieving of the goal. For most teams, the team leader is very precise in choosing whom he/she wants on the team, so readers and audiences are usually very clear about who is doing what and why. But, just because it's obvious that this is important, never assume a large cast of characters will have everyone maximizing his or her roles in an entertaining and functional way.

Every member has a developmental stage role to fulfill.

This is a role characteristic that most are not familiar with, because they are not aware of team stages. But, in each stage of development (forming, storming, norming, performing) each team member provides a specific team function in that stage. This is a complicated topic, and we cannot define each role for each stage here, but know that there are at least nine different roles that characters can play in each of the four stages. In other words, there are some 36 different roles that characters can play in a team, based on their personality style, and the stage they occupy at any one point in the team's development. Knowing these developmental roles helps you deepen every character so that they are not just one-dimensional, cookie cutters straight out of central casting (i.e., plucky comic relief, sexy vixen, geeky brainiac, etc.).

I realize it's a bit of a tease to reveal this idea of roles without going into more detail, but the can of worms I would be opening, if I did so, would make this e-book far too unwieldy. Consequently, I will only suggest that you check out this topic in my forthcoming book, *Rapid Story Development: How to Use the Enneagram-Story Connection to Become a Masterful Storyteller* (Focal Press), where I will break down all nine of the personality styles involved, along with each team developmental role by stage, and give suggestions on how to leverage each in the writing process.

Some members provide a window into the main character's personal situation.

In many ways, this is the hardest feature of team roles to accomplish. As with subplots, characters in stories are more than just plot devices. They are dramatic windows into the protagonist's character. The term "supporting character" means something specific. A supporting character *supports* the main character. What this means is that they help the hero or heroine move through the mainline story in such a way that the reader or viewer learns more about who they are because of this other character's presence and participation. Through their own character moments, the supporting character becomes a window into a deeper view of why the protagonist is acting a particular way or feeling a particular feeling.

Every character in a story need not play this reflective role, but certainly, the central characters of any story need to do so, and in a team story that means the other team members. Again, perhaps not every team member, especially if the team is large (ala *Oceans 11*), but there should be several window-characters on any team to help readers or audiences better understand the motivations and actions of the protagonist (which is usually the team leader).

In addition to roles mentioned above, one last consideration is that supporting characters can also act as a kind of Greek Chorus. In classical theater, the Greek Chorus served to articulate or express outright moral issues in a story or reflect on emotional action unfolding at various points in a play's performance. Similarly, in team stories, supporting characters (or even individual characters) can act as a literal window into the mind and emotional state of the protagonist, functioning as a chorus to reveal to the audience or reader new windows of understanding into the issues facing the hero or heroine and their inner angst, concerns, or feelings as they work through dramatic conflict.

EXAMPLE: TEAM-BASED STORY

Let's apply what we've just covered to a real-world example of a story that is well established and regarded in theater, film, and television. In this example, I'll highlight each of the team characteristics and explain how they play out specifically in the story, in order to show that this is not just some abstract application, but reflects how great stories are written.

Example:

12 *Angry Men* (Writer Reginald Rose play/screenplay, 1957 – United Artists)

#*1: A PROTAGONIST CARRIES THE STORY*

Juror #8 (Henry Fonda). This character carries the narrative and drives the story.

#2: *Story is focused on a single main goal/task*

The team goal/task is to come to a verdict.

#3: *Plot is time sensitive*

There is no specific timeframe set, but the pressure is to do it as soon as possible.

#4: *Subplots are in service to the mainline story*

All the various power plays, manipulations, etc. between jury members are all focused on making decisions to accommodate either Juror #3 (Lee J. Cobb) or Juror #8 (the antagonism between these two characters is the mainline story). Alliances are formed, opposition solidified, and all of it is designed to force Juror #8 to get off the dime and vote "guilty," so they can all go home and be done. Unfortunately, Juror #8 will not comply.

#5: *Stories develop in stages that build dramatic cohesion*

Forming Stage: The jury takes a little bit of time get to know one another; the jury foreman sets the agenda, and the honeymoon is over pretty quickly when the first vote is taken and Juror #8 votes "not guilty" against all the others' "guilty."

Storming Stage: The jury spends most of the story in this stage. Each character reveals specific personality styles that contribute to the forward or backward motion of the decision-making process, and; Juror #3 emerges quickly as the driving opposition to force Juror #8 to conform to the team's "guilty" majority.

Norming Stage: This stage gradually emerges in the form of side conversations, little side vignettes where various jurors reveal their prejudices, peculiarities, and vicissitudes; and where Juror #8 slowly starts to cast doubt about the defendant's guilt, slowly winning over more and more jurors to his position, inexorably turning the tables on Juror #3.

Performing Stage: This stage is represented by an almost total reversal of fortune for Juror #3, with him standing alone in the end as the sole "guilty" voter, and the entire team now working together to support Juror #8. The team is performing as a unified whole against Juror #3, as a result of the steadfast refusal of Juror #8 to give in to Juror #3's threats and harangues. The transformation of the team from a bickering, squabbling, and backstabbing amalgam into a real team operating out of common agreements and aligned goals (lets all vote "not guilty") is complete when Juror #3 is forced by peer pressure to back down and "go along" with the majority decision to vote "not guilty."

6: *Stories tend to be continuous, not episodic.*

The story has minor subplots occurring around the table, but these are more like side discussion, not really subplots. Over all, the story is one continuous dramatic narrative, not a jumble of episodic moments strung together like pearls on a narrative string (e.g., an ensemble story).

SUMMARY

As you can see, there are a great many factors that come into play when assessing a story idea whether it falls into the team category. What you will find as you test out these ideas in your own stories is that some will apply easily and obviously, while others may be more difficult to fit into some scenarios. The stages of development are usually the elements that will either jump out as applicable or struggle for relevancy. While I said earlier if you have a team story you will have stages of development because all teams go through these stages, there will nonetheless be those stories where the stages will play out along a continuum from very present to barely present, but they will be there, however weakly structured.

This is the takeaway: *don't force it.* The entire exercise of developing a team story is not meant to force any story into some cookie cutter. There will be stories that have many of the team characteristics, but there will be others that fall short. This is not bad or wrong, it just is the way it is. You and your story will both be better off for the process, however. Apply the definitions, apply the characteristics, do the analysis, then whatever decisions you come to about how you want to build your team story will be conscious, well informed, and productive not because you blindly followed someone's directions—no, rather because you entered into the development process with your eyes wide open and made your own decisions and found your own development path. Even if your team story doesn't meet all the check marks on the checklist, it will meet many or most of them.

-----

[1] "team." BusinessDictionary.com. WebFinance, Inc. http://www.businessdictionary.com/definition/team.html (accessed: October 20, 2018).

[2] Based on a larger conceptual model defined in "Development Sequence in Small Groups" by Bruce Tuckman, Prof. of Education at Ohio University, 1965.

THE ENSEMBLE STORY

When most writers consider the idea of an ensemble story they think like playwrights, meaning they define "ensemble" the way they do in the theater:

> 66 ... an approach to acting that aims for a unified effect achieved by all members of a cast working together on behalf of the play, rather than emphasizing individual performances." [1]

An ensemble is a reference to the players and how they serve the piece (play) through their function as actors. In many respects, this idea of ensemble is very team-like in its meaning: a group of people working together to accomplish a specific goal.

It so happens that this theater definition of an ensemble is not far from the truth for writers of other forms. The characters (actors) of a story are in service to the story, not the other way around. Characters in a piece of fictional prose exist to help tell the story and shed light upon the experience of the protagonist, who is the center of the story universe.

But, the theater definition of ensemble, while barking up the right stage prop tree, is nonetheless short of the mark. The structure of the ensemble in theater is seen collectively as a kind of community. In its purest form, however, the ensemble is in actuality just the opposite. Rather than holding the spirit of "one for all, and all for one," the real call to action for ensembles is "every man for himself."

THE TYRANNY OF THE PROTAGONIST

Hollywood is probably responsible, more than any other source, for the ascendency of the protagonist. The novel certainly emphasizes the centrality of the protagonist in any dramatic situation, but the novel (or long form prose in general) often dilutes or diverges from the protagonist-centric story to explore less linear approaches.

Film, however, for the bulk of its century-plus existence has obsessively held to the protagonist model of storytelling. So much so, that it is by far the favored form of storytelling by most artists. But, even film had its experimenters. D. W. Griffith, in 1916, introduced one of the first purely ensemble forms of filmmaking with his epic *Intolerance*. Spanning some twenty-five-hundred years, the film tells four separate stories, each with its own protagonist and storyline, and yet connected through the use of time itself, with the help of editing techniques like cross-cutting. Griffith also used the recurring image of a woman rocking a cradle as a unifying metaphor to show how each story related to the whole, connected through time by the passing of generations.

Knowing or unknowingly, Griffiths's brilliant storytelling, and abandonment of the main protagonist model, became highly influential among European filmmakers at the time, likely contributing to the establishment of the later so-called "European sensibility." As we shall see later on, *Intolerance* exhibits all the core characteristics of a pure ensemble story and, in that context, represents a prototype for the form.

TELEVISION

There is probably no medium better suited for ensemble writing than television. TV shows allow for the flexibility of writers to change point of view weekly; focus on different characters in separate episodes of a series; tell multiple storylines simultaneously across a large story space, which may or may not allow for individual story intersections.

Ensemble storytelling with casts of twenty or more actors is common in American soap operas and Spanish-language telenovelas, genres that require continuous expansion of storylines and casts as a series evolves. All you have to do is look at the longevity of some of these shows (*General Hospital*, UK's *Coronation Street*, *La Patrona*) to see how this form of storytelling is not just sustainable, but popular with audiences.

SO, WHAT EXACTLY IS AN ENSEMBLE STORY?

An ensemble story is an assembly of multiple storylines which may or may not intersect one another, but are instead connected based upon some organizing idea-theme such as love, happiness, race, forgiveness, etc. (e.g., *Crash* (2004), *The Big Chill* (1983), *Thirteen Conversations About One Thing* (2001)), or a physical design element such as a setting, an event, or a symbol (e.g., *New Year's Eve* (2001), *Valentines Day* (2010), *Contagion* (2011)).

Ensemble stories walk a strange line, balancing characters who may be total strangers, but at the same time giving the impression of interconnectedness between them. The theory of "six degrees of separation" is a theory that definitely applies to ensembles. This theory was proposed by Hungarian author Frigyes Karinthy in 1929 and suggests that any two people on the planet are connected by no more than six separate steps. In other words, we're all connected, regardless of how unknown we may be to one another. Ensemble stories live and breath by this idea, and leverage many devices (theme, physicality, location, metaphor) to support this feeling of connectedness between characters.

In ensemble stories, individual characters act out their personal lives giving different perspectives of the organizing idea-theme of the story; and the degree to which there is any resolution among the competing perspectives is what determines the power and effectiveness of the story on the audience or reader.

The central distinction, however, is that ensemble stories do not support a single, key throughline featuring a main protagonist. These are stories where there are three or more characters carrying the weight of the drama as equally as possible. They are very hard to write well, but there are many fine examples where playwrights, screenwriters, and novelists have weaved multiple, dense, and powerful narratives together in this fashion —often not having any of them directly touch one another— while still managing to keep viewing audiences and readers focused and engaged.

The great beauty of ensemble stories is that by taking away the focus on a single protagonist, they give the writer the ability to emphasize the interactions between characters based on controlling ideas, thus giving readers and audiences multiple windows into the story, rather than just one. The great danger with ensemble pieces is that they can result in works that lack a dramatic center of attention and narrative drive. With no main character acting as the center of the dramatic storm, something must unite the other characters so that there is a sense of narrative unity, purpose, and flow.

The challenge for the writer lies in finding that unifying theme, idea, or physical component that can help the reader or audience stay focused and engaged. So, while in most cases having a single protagonist is the soundest, and most satisfying way to tell a story, the ensemble story can also deliver an effective and powerful experience when executed by a masterful storyteller.

Novelists (and TV series writers) are in the best possible position when it comes to writing ensemble stories, compared with feature screenwriters or even playwrights. Why is it easier for novelists to execute the ensemble? The answer is simple, something I call "story real estate."

Novelists have no constraints when it comes to writing a book. There are no limits, besides those imposed by publishers for their various imprints. Basically, novelists do what they want. The canvas is broad and expands endlessly. One recent example of this is the smash-hit, autobiographical series by Norwegian author Karl Ove Knausgarrd, *My Struggle*, some three-thousand-six-hundred pages across six volumes.

Screenwriters have no such luxury. For example, feature screenplays have an artificial ceiling of 120 pages (more like 110 pages for most genre films) and in television, half-hour sitcoms are only about 22 pages. Story real estate is cramped and costly for screenwriters. Think of it this way: screenwriters live in a tiny, two-tatami-mat micro apartment in Tokyo; and novelists live on a five-thousand-acre cattle ranch in Montana. Screenwriters and playwrights don't have the story real estate to juggle multiple characters the way a novelist can.

That said, there are those exceptions in television like Rainer Werner Fassbinder's *Berlin Alexanderplatz*, a sprawling 14-part mini-series based on the German novel of the same name, and in theater August Wilson's Pittsburgh Cycle of ten plays. The point is that writers, generally, do not write thousands of pages or tens of volumes when they create a "piece" of prose. The outliers do not create best practices in any art, they are merely the exceptional exceptions that the rest of us try to emulate.

Consider the real-world example of the fantasy series *A Song of Ice and Fire* (Random House), by George R. R. Martin. In each book of the seven-part series, some volumes being over one thousand pages, many characters share equal story space and time telling their individual tales. Readers love the series, and Martin's ensemble-writing style works because he can take as long as he likes to pull readers in and luxuriate in character details, backstories, changing emotional states, and grizzly goings-on of palace intrigue.

Over the years, one of the reasons Martin resisted attempts by film producers to turn his series into a feature film was that he didn't think a two-hour format could do justice to his books. And coming from the world of television writing himself (*Beauty and the Beast, Twilight Zone, The Outer Limits*), he knew his concern was justified. It was only after the *Game of Thrones* (HBO) producers, Dan Weiss and David Benioff, shared their vision for a multi-season, serialized vision of his books that Martin agreed to let *A Song of Ice and Fire* to be adapted for television. The serialized, limited series, and miniseries formats that are now popular with primetime, streaming, and cable networks afford producers and writers the same broad canvas as novelists to give television audiences immersive and complex story worlds. In this serial/series environment, ensemble stories flourish and make for great entertainment—and some great writing, all thanks to the long-form, novelistic format provided by expanded story real estate.

Regardless of how much or little story real estate you might be working with, any ensemble story will feel cumbersome and overblown if the story's action and conflict are occurring out of creative whims or flights of writer fancy; meaning, the writer throws in action scenes, or character conflict, or dazzling set pieces because they think it would be cool to do so. In other words, there is no valid story reason to add the content, it's just a caprice on the part of the writer.

When dramatic content is added to any story, ensemble or otherwise, it must always source from characters themselves and their motivations, desires, and moral blind spots (see my e-book *Rapid Story Development #5: The Moral Premise–How to Build a Bulletproof Narrative Engine for any Story*), otherwise the story will become defocused and slowly wander off on dramatic tangents and pointless digressions. Once again, George R. R. Martin's *A Song of Ice and Fire* is a wonderful example of how to write a massive tome of a series, while keeping all the action and conflict rooted in character flaws and personal conflict, while maintaining thematic interconnectedness throughout all subplots and the mainline plot, with almost no padding or dramatic fluff. I highly recommend studying this series to see how a master craftsman executed not just a brilliant piece of entertaining writing, but also as a master class in ensemble storytelling.

Ensemble Definition for Writers

While the ensemble definition offered at the beginning of this chapter is technically accurate for defining an ensemble in a community of actors, it is not perhaps the best definition for creative writers. So, let me present an alternative definition of an ensemble that you can use in developing your own ensemble stories.

An ensemble in fictional stories is defined as:

1. A collection of three or more characters with a loose or nonexistent personal connection,

- none of whom can be singled out as a central protagonist,
- and pursuing separate personal story goals/desires,
- but collectively making a shared narrative statement about the human condition,
- that is in service to the overall achievement of telling a story.

2. Ensemble members:

- operate along dramatically independent lines,
- interact only at the level of theme, idea, or some other level of narrative abstraction,
- share collectively in communicating the overall narrative message of a story,

- but do so without the presence of a continuous, cause-and-effect driven mainline narrative.

There are no doubt many examples of stories you can think of that fall somewhere inside, or outside, of this definition. As with the team-story definition, this one is not meant to be a "law" that is unbreakable. It is only a guideline to use when developing an ensemble story. But, if you are doing so, and the story at hand is going to be a pure form of the ensemble, then this definition will be invaluable in guiding you into the right development approach.

As I said earlier, in the chapter "The Gray Zone" we will look at several examples of ensemble stories that straddle some parts of this definition, and downright ignore other parts, and yet may still retain more of an ensemble feel when all factors are examined. The point is that you as the writer need useful tools to do this examining so that you don't have to wing it and settle for the best guesstimate. This definition offered above, and the next section will give you those tools, and point your nose accordingly.

Ensemble Characteristics

Like team stories, ensemble stories have specific characteristics that distinguish them from other story forms. There are six basic characteristics that are almost always present in any ensemble story:

Ensemble Characteristics
All main characters have equal dramatic weight
The story is defocused on multiple goals/tasks
The plot may or may not be time sensitive
Subplots serve a broader context, not a main plot
Develops along independent lines, not stages
Story lines are almost always episodic, not continuous

As with the team story characteristics, I don't want to spend a lot of time here detailing ensemble characteristic here, as we will revisit each of these in a couple of chapters in more detail, but some of these also need a little explanation.

All main characters have an equal dramatic weight.

What this basically means is that the main characters (i.e, those characters who carry the responsibility for telling the main storylines), do not stand out enough to dominate the dramatic landscape of the overall piece. There is no main character (as in a team story), only main *characters*.

The story is defocused on multiple goals/tasks.

There is no single story goal for the piece. Each individual story in the overall narrative may have a focused goal, but the narrative as a single presentation does not. This is a major factor in adding to the episodic character of ensemble stories.

The plot may or may not be time sensitive (usually not).

There may be a ticking clock used to drive the overall narrative, or individual stories inside the bigger whole, but this is rare. If so, this is a unifying abstraction (see definition) to create a sense of relatedness and not necessarily a key plotting device to raise interdependence across all characters.

Subplots serve a broader context, not a mainline plot.

Individual, episodic stories within the whole narrative are not in service to some main plot or protagonist, but only loosely to the high-level story context/message. This is in contrast to a team story where subplots support the protagonist's storyline.

Develops along independent lines, not stages.

This refers to the above references to subplots and there being no mainline story. Individual characters "run" their own storylines and they typically unfold in isolation of one another. There are no team-like stages involved, only the normal genre beats that may be associated with the main story's genre.

Storylines are almost always episodic, not continuous.

Also relating back to earlier comments about independent lines, no mainline story, etc. this means that episodic writing is inherently necessary in ensemble stories, because there will invariably be multiple story goals, multiple opposition structures, and multiple "main" characters.

EXAMPLE: ENSEMBLE STORY

13 Conversations About One Thing (Writers Karen and Jill Sprecher, 2001 – Sony Pictures Classics)

#1: *ALL MAIN CHARACTERS HAVE EQUAL DRAMATIC WEIGHT*

Multiple characters, all with their own separate struggles and challenges, grapple with the twists and downturns of human happiness and the randomness of life.

Troy (Matthew McConauhey) is an assistant prosecutor high on life, who carelessly hits a pedestrian while happily drunk, and thinking he's killed her finds his own happiness spiralling away into a hole of guilt and self-loathing.

Gene (Alan Arkin) a mid-level manager, and pessimistic about the possibility of real happiness, fires the happiest guy in his department because he sees the upside of everything, good or bad. Gene can't stomach what he sees as pie-in-the-sky happiness, and this eats away at him.

Walker (John Turturro) is a sardonic college professor who cheats on his wife (Amy Irving) with a woman (Barbara Sukowa), who realizes Walker is just going through the motions because he's been told this is how to find happiness.

And a maid (Clea DuVall) who loves her work, but works for a Grinch who only complains and criticizes. The maid is randomly injured and suffers great pain that she clearly doesn't deserve.

#2: *STORY IS DEFOCUSED ON MULTIPLE GOALS/TASKS*

Each main character has his/her own problem to solve, emotional challenge, and sometimes diffuse desire to achieve. Troy wants to be punished for being too happy and for his crime; Gene wants desperately to understand why he can't be happy in the face of others' happiness; Walker is just clueless about what happiness means; and the maid can't understand why bad things happen to good, happy people, such as herself.

#3: *PLOT MAY OR MAY NOT BE TIME SENSITIVE*

There is no timeframe or time pressure.

#4: *SUBPLOTS SERVE A BROADER CONTEXT, NOT A MAINLINE STORY*

There is no mainline story, but all the storylines are connected by topic/theme: happiness, it's randomness, and life being a total crapshoot.

#5: *STORIES DEVELOP ALONG INDEPENDENT LINES, NOT STAGES*

Each story stands alone but is vaguely connected to all the other stories through the bigger thematic context. There is nothing to form, storm, norm, or perform. In the context of an ensemble setup, these terms have no meaning.

6: *STORIES LINES ARE MOSTLY EPISODIC, NOT CONTINUOUS.*

Each of the different story lines run in parallel and are not dramatically interdependent as stories, but they do possess a contractural connection that gives the overall story a coherent feel. Mostly, however, the effect is episodic, not continuous.

SUMMARY

Like team stories, ensemble stories are complex and subtle things. Ensemble stories in many ways present flexible and creative opportunities to tell sophisticated and engaging stories, but they also create many traps and hairpin turns which might derail the development process.

This is why knowing all these definitions, characteristics, and process questions are an advantage to any writer. You have a roadmap for analysis and decision making. Ensemble stories are probably the most dangerous forms of stories to enter into blindly, without a map you will get lost.

Also, as with team stories, ensemble stories abhor a cookie cutter. Do not slavishly apply all this information to your stories expecting crystal clear and bright, shiny answers every time you get to work. There will be those stories that fall into line and effortlessly cooperate, but there will be others that resist; those scenarios and characters who push back on one or more of the characteristics—*great*! This means the creative process is exerting itself and you are being original in your writing. Listen to your process and keep moving through the analysis and application. If you have an ensemble story it will emerge out of the work. If you don't, the same work will make that clear. Either way, you will be better off and will have one more experience that validates the idea that conscious writing is better than winging it and hoping everything will just turn out okay.

----

[1] www.dictionary.com. (2018). *the definition of ensemble acting.* [online] Available at: https://www.dictionary.com/browse/ensemble-acting [Accessed 11 Oct. 2018].

TEAM & ENSEMBLE STORIES

COMPARE & CONTRAST

Allow me to state up front that this book is entirely focused on the concept of teams, not ensembles. The whole idea of this e-book is to demonstrate the natural fit team development has within the function of telling a story. Ensembles are an essential part of this discussion because that's what most people think they are writing when they write a story with a large cast. This is sometimes true, but most times not sure.

As a writer, you need the craft skills to know what you are dealing with when it is in front of you, but when you don't know what you don't know you are going to do the best you can with what you've got: meant, you will wing it. The reality is that most stories fall into the team subset, not the ensemble subset. But until you know how and why that is the case, you are setting yourself up to do one thing (write a cool story with a big cast), but end up doing something else (write a cool story with the wrong structure and muddy it all up).

This is why we must now look at what the distinctions are between these two subsets of genre presentation so that you can know going in what you are dealing with, so you can make informed and powerful development decisions along the way.

LOOKING UNDER THE HOOD

Understanding the central distinctions between ensemble stories and team stories is an essential story development skill every writer needs to develop. As forms, teams are not better than ensembles, they each serve different development purposes. The story structure, writing approach, and narrative design for each follow very different paths depending on which story form a writer chooses.

Which one you pick depends on your story goals and personal peccadilloes for designing and delivering a chosen narrative. Either way, knowing what you are writing, and why you are writing it are crucial. How conscious are you about your writing goals and objectives?

To that end, consider the table below that compares and contrasts the 12 basic characteristics of ensemble stories and team stories. We reviewed these twelve characteristics in the previous chapters, but here you can see them side-by-side. Seeing them in this way helps to contrast their fundamental differences, but also helps to give you some perspective on why they are both effective in what they do best while demanding very different story approaches.

TEAM VS. ENSEMBLE STORY CHARACTERISTICS

Teams	vs.	Ensembles
A protagonist carries the story		All main characters have equal dramatic weight
The story is focused on a single main goal/task		The story is defocused on multiple goals/tasks
The plot is time sensitive		The plot may or may not be time sensitive
Subplots are at service to the mainline story		Subplots serve a broader context, not a main plot
Develops in stages that build dramatic cohesion		Develops along independent lines, not stages
Story lines tend to be continuous, not episodic		Story lines are almost always episodic, not continuous

COMPARE & CONTRAST

1. A *protagonist carries the story* vs. *All main characters have equal dramatic weight.*

In a team story, you have a central character driving the story. One character is clearly standing front-and-center as the emotional and dramatic focus, with all the emotional action spinning around him/her (12 *Angry Men, The Expendables,* 2001 *A Space Odyssey*). With ensemble stories, just the opposite is true. Various characters step front-and-center, then recede into the background to give other character stories their centerstage moment.

Eventually, all the stories converge or resolve around some idea, incident, theme, or symbol (*Crash, 13 Conversations About One Thing, Grand Canyon*). The classic idea of the hero/heroine-centric story is abandoned in an ensemble story but embraced fully in the team format.

2. *Story is focused on a single main goal/task vs. Story is defocused on multiple goals/tasks.*

In team-based stories, since you have a protagonist driving the mainline story, there will be a protagonist-driven goal or desire that will need to be achieved by the end. This is a basic story structure requirement of classic story development. The hero/heroine's purpose or drive sets the agenda for the team (*Ocean's Eleven, The Dirty Dozen, Predator*).

Consequently, in team stories, the actions taken to achieve the story/team goal are inherently cause-and-effect oriented. This means that the ultimate story goal is dependent on a series of minor or subordinate goals being achieved, which in aggregate make it possible for the protagonist and team to achieve their desired outcome.

In ensemble stories, however, there is no such focus or cause and effect relationship with story action. Rather than a single focus, there are many foci, many tasks, many goals, and they may or may not coalesce in some neat and tidy way (*Intolerance, The Yellow Rolls Royce, The Big Chill*).

When handled badly, this lack of focused goal setting can lead to disjointed storytelling and fragmented development, but when handled well can lead to subtle and complex layers of narrative that build on one another like artful mosaics (*The Red Violin; Manhattan Tales; Paris, je t'aime*)

3. *Plot is time sensitive vs. Plot may or may not be time sensitive (usually not).*

Team stories typically have a ticking clock of some kind operating across the span of the story, while ensemble stories do not. There may be a sense of urgency or pressure, but ensemble stories usually do not have time constraints in the same way as team-based stories.

In team stories, the normal storyline plays out over established "story-time," meaning the linear timeframe needed to tell the story within whatever time period the story is set. In an ensemble story, however, time can be used in the same way as in a team story, or in multiple other ways.

Ticking clock: In an ensemble story you can have a ticking clock to create the same sense of story pressure and tension as in a team story, but this is not the norm. The film *Contagion* is a good example of a story that is largely an ensemble piece and that uses a ticking clock (the spread of a deadly disease). *Contagion* is a real mishmash of forms (part team, part ensemble) and we'll examine it more closely in the last chapter, but it is primarily an ensemble story that uses time in the same way a team story does.

Thematic Connector: Time as a thematic connector refers to

stories that have time or its passing as a general thematic message throughout the story. The old silent film *Intolerance* falls into this category of time usage. As I described it in the previous chapter, *Intolerance* uses time thematically to make a statement about the passing of generations and with each generation the steadfastness of hatred and intolerance. The clock is not ticking in a suspenseful way, but it is passing in a relentless way, with Eternal Motherhood (Lilian Gish) acting as the glue that gives the cycle of human life and death (time) continuity.

Physical plotting device: Time as plotting device refers to the usage of time not in an abstract form to send a message, but as a practical story beat to tell the story. *The Red Violin* is a good example of a story that uses time in a powerful way to move actual story segments forward, building toward some culmination (the final auction of the violin). Separate stories connected by the violin itself unfold in a pure ensemble way, but time has a very concrete plot role to play, as distinct from a story like *Intolerance.*

The larger point here about time is that in a team story-time has a fairly standard default usage (linear timeline, set within story-time), but ensemble stories have no such default, and in that sense ensembles may be more flexible in how they approach the problem of time.

4. Subplots are in service to the mainline story vs. Subplots serve a broader context, not a mainline story.

Subplots are a complicated and broad subject area, and I discuss them in more detail in my upcoming e-book, *Rapid Story Devel-*

opment: How to Write Subplots and Supporting Characters that Work, but for now know that in any story that has a single main character and mainline story, subplots are in service the mainline story; i.e., the story of the protagonist.

In a story, subplots are added windows into the protagonist's journey. They stand alone as "mini-stories" along with the mainline story, but they should reflect the journey of the hero-heroine as closely as possible, not act separately as full stories in and of themselves.

In other words, a subplot is "sub" (i.e., subordinate) to some "plot," not an isolated story within the story of some main character. Subplots are very hard to pull off, and most writers fail at this distinction in their writing, but when subplots are structured properly the entire story benefits and the mainline story (protagonist's line) takes on even more power and effectiveness. Team-based stories follow this "rule" about subplots.

Ensemble stories typically do not; each storyline has its own standalone trajectory, and all these mini-stories don't even have to intersect or connect for the overall narrative to work. Sometimes they do in ensemble pieces, but they don't have to. Every character tells their own story and there is a sense of narrative cohesion because they are all connected thematically, physically, symbolically, or in some other tangible way. In ensemble stories there are no subplots, there are only individual mini-stories loosely or closely connected by some device other than a central protagonist.

5. *Stories develop in stages that build dramatic cohesion vs. Stories develop along independent lines, not stages.*

As stated earlier, teams form in stages (*forming, storming, norming, performing*) and team-based stories follow this pattern. Why? Because all teams follow this pattern, real or fictional. As a writer, you don't have to do anything—there are no rules—but there is a consequence to not following the real-world principles of team development in fictional scenarios.

The consequence is that the fictional team will not feel as natural, coherent, or dramatically interconnected if you ignore the normal stages of team development. If that is okay with you, then have fun, just know readers and viewing audiences will viscerally know the difference between a team-based story that follows a natural development and one that ignores it. Team stories that ignore the natural dynamics of team stages will feel flat, forced, predictable, and boring; and readers and viewing audiences will pick up on these weaknesses immediately, regardless of how masterful the writer or director might be in their craft.

Ensemble stories, on the other hand, follow the normal story structure patterns of natural storytelling (like any story), but they do not follow any stages. There is no "natural" line of development for an ensemble story, there are only the universal elements of classic story structure, which rule any story, regardless of form, and the usual story beats that follow each individual genre.

6. storylines tend to be continuous, not episodic vs. storylines are almost always episodic, not continuous.

Episodic writing and continuous writing are not story development issues, they are more about writing style and not story form. But they are important in terms of how a story is told on the page or screen. In poorly told team stories there can definitely be episodic writing that breaks up what should be a continuous storyline, but this is not some mark of clever storytelling, rather it is a mark of poor writing.

Episodic writing can have many causes:

<u>Multiple opponents</u>: In these kinds of stories, the hero/heroine (or the team) come up against distinctly different opponents as they move through the mainline story. Each opponent is defeated and the team moves on to the next challenge (*Jason and the Argonauts*). Each opponent has its own goal (beat the opponent) and stands alone with its own storyline with a beginning, middle, and an end. Readers or audiences are then subjected to many starts and stops in the narrative, which may or may not be too distracting overall.

<u>*Mini-stories within stories*</u>: More than just multiple opponents, mini-stories can present full-blown stories within a larger narrative. These mini-stories have their own protagonists, opposition, moral components, etc. and often find themselves competing with the mainline story within which they are being told. Sometimes they can be brilliantly delivered so that they do not overpower the mainline story, but most often they detract, not add to, the read.

Split stories: These are stories where the protagonist starts off wanting one thing but then changes their goal midway through the story. This can often lead to splitting not just the goal of the hero/heroine, but also adding new opposition structures (multiple opponents) that complicate the matter. Split stories are very common in prose fiction, and they seldom are pulled off successful. Most often they kill pace and dissipate dramatic tension, thus undermining the overall narrative.

Split protagonists: This is a version of split stories, but takes the form of changing main characters midstream. The story starts off following one person, then, at some point (usually in the middle) shifts to another person's story through to the conclusion. A good example of this in film is the movie *The Prestige*. This story follows two magicians and almost divides the storytelling evenly between them. It attempts to connect everything in the end by bringing each of the men's stories full circle, but the reality is that splitting protagonists divides not just the audience's attention, but also story-time. Think about it: if you split your protagonists then you have half as much time to develop either one of them, as opposed to having only one hero/heroine and taking a whole book or movie to focus on one main character. This is a common error with amateur writers, but can still occur with experienced writers.

The upshot of all these causes of episodic writing is that stories can become plagued by fits and starts, distractions, mangled pacing, and blow opportunities to keep up the dramatic pressure.

When team stories come off feeling episodic, it is usually

because of poor writing. But, when ensemble stories come off as episodic, it is more often due to the nature of an ensemble story, not bad writing. Remember, ensemble stories are made up of isolated storylines that are connected through themes, symbols, locations, etc., consequently episodic writing will be inherently part of the writing. It is unavoidable. I some ways this forces the writer to compensate with clever writing and solid storytelling so that the overall pace and dramatic tension are maintained. This is another reason why ensemble stories are so hard to write, but also so satisfying when they are written well (*13 Conversations About One Thing*, Sony Pictures Classics).

HOW DO YOU KNOW WHEN YOU HAVE A TEAM OR ENSEMBLE STORY?

It's all fine and good to have definitions you can work with and lists of characteristics you can double-check, but how do all these best practices help you decide what to do when you have a story idea? Should you write a team story? Should you write an ensemble story? Should the story be some mix of the two? Is mixing them even an option?

Theoretical ideas are fairly useless unless they lead to practical applications. So, let's talk about application and how you turn all this information into an action plan that can inform your actual process.

HOW TO DETERMINE IF YOUR STORY IS A TEAM STORY

The obvious test question for this issue is: does the idea fit the team definition? Not a bad place to start, but the problem with relying solely on the team definition is that most writers will have story ideas in their heads that straddle both definitions (team and ensemble). This is not intentional, but this is what happens, more than not.

Stories are messy. They don't like cookie cutters, or paradigms, or rulebooks. They go where they want to go (not really, you take them where you want them to go, but it feels like that sometimes). We're going to look at this phenomenon in the last chapter, "The Gray Zone," as we examine known stories that cross definitions, mix characteristics, and defy easy identification. But, even these stories can be nailed down by asking many of the questions you are going to learn now. When you know the right questions to ask, just about anything is understandable.

(NOTE: *Try not to be put off with some of the information that follows if it feels a little repetitive from the previous chapter; it is. But, I think this is a good thing, as more exposure to these concepts—in context—will only deepen your absorption of the principles and ideas.*)

Team Story Questions:

1. *Is there a protagonist?*

Do you have a protagonist or not? Can you easily identify who is driving the central narrative? The protagonist is usually the character who sets everything in motion, dramatically speaking, and who has a specific goal they are trying to achieve, and who recruits others to help them pursue this goal as the narrative unfolds.

The "sense" of a protagonist is not some airy-fairy impression, it is not amorphous, it is not vague. You know them and you can viscerally feel them within your idea. This is important, so let me repeat it: you can know you have a protagonist just by the idea you have, you don't have to have a fully (or partially) developed story.

Only those writers who fly by the seats of their pants and sit back and wait for the story to tell them what the story is about, or who are the main characters, are the ones who struggle with this question. If you master the basic process of premise and story development you will *never* have this issue. But, let's say you do. Let's say you can't tell who your protagonist is in your idea or story. Easy, just ask these three simple questions:

- Who has the most to lose?
- Who is in the most pain, emotionally?
- Who changes the most in the end?

One character will always satisfy these three questions. If, for some reason, you still can't know who your protagonist is, then this is a sign that you probably have an ensemble story. Not bad or wrong, just not a team story. So, take note of this and move on.

When you can identify that you have a protagonist, that is the first big red flag that you have a team story.

2. *Is there a single story goal?*

Does the development and evolution of the story revolve around a central goal being achieved? Is the world saved? Does the boy get the girl (or boy)? Does the murder get solved? Does the monster get killed? Does the teenager come of age? I think you get the idea. The story goal is what you have been reading about and watching in movies and on TV your whole life. It is the "thing" that has to happen, or begotten, or uncovered, etc. by the end of the story, and usually is the result of some protagonist being on a mission.

What happens to many writers, however as they wrestle with this question in their stories, is that they experience many false starts before they land on the real goal. If that happens to you, that's okay, just keep playing with your idea until the singular goal emerges. It will be obvious if you have a team story, and it will almost always be connected at the hip to your protagonist's personal story.

If you find it, then this is the second, big red flag that you have a team story.

3. Are there stages of development?

This question is less intuitive than the first two. In order to answer it, you need to be familiar with the concept of team stages of development. This is not a common subject most writers have had exposure to, so it is not surprising that many will fumble on this one. But, this can be expected, because there are moments in every story where people argue and fight (storming stage), and agree and come together (norming stage), etc. Even in ensemble stories, there will be moments like these that might suggest stages, but upon closer examination, they will not be there.

If you have a team story the stages will be obvious, they will be more than quick moments or scenes passing by, and they will wax and wane. What this means is that a team will start to storm, get through this stage, start to norm, then blow up again and regress back to storming, finally moving back to norming, and so on. Teams in life do this all the time, and so do fictional teams.

The key to look for is significant sections of the story where the characters live in these stages and/or wax and wane, back and forth through them through story-time. This means stages are occurring. Similarly, they will not start with performing and end up on forming (stage 4 and stage 1), the progression will always be linear from forming to performing (stage 1 to 4). In ensemble stories, you may have vague impressions of storming or forming moments but the stages are not real and do not exist.

If you determine that team stages are clearly present in your story, then this is the third big red flag you have a team story.

4. Is the mainline story one continuous dramatic narrative?

Team stories flow in a linear, cause-and-effect path that has a beginning, a middle, and an end. Subplots might break up this path from time to time, but if subplots are properly developed they will enhance, not detract from the mainline story's flow.

This may sound obvious and simplistic, but you would be surprised how often writers fall into the quicksand of episodic writing (see the previous chapter). Team stories are not episodic, they are continuous, and if they feel episodic it is because the writer is trying to consciously achieve this effect for some dramatic reason, or they are unconscious and have stumbled into the quicksand.

If the story follows a continuous and interconnected narrative, and especially if subplots support that narrative, then this is the last big red flag you have a team story.

HOW TO DETERMINE IF YOUR STORY IS AN ENSEMBLE STORY

Just as with team stories, ensemble stories can be determined by asking a few strategically relevant questions. In some ways, the questions you ask for ensembles are a bit less direct than with team stories, but they will still get you where you want to go, i.e., in a position to make a decision.

Ensemble Story Questions:

1. Is it hard to decide on one central protagonist?

When you think about your characters, do they all feel like they could qualify as a central protagonist? When you ask the three basic questions about who is in the most pain, who has the most to lose, and who changes the most in the end, do you find yourself saying, "Gosh, they all are in pain, have something to lose, and change in the end."?

What will probably happen is not some equivalence between each character, meaning they all won't literally feel equal in every area of emotion, stakes, or growth, but they will be compelling enough in these qualities to make you stop and think.

I this is the case, then this is the first big red flag you have an ensemble story.

2. Is it unclear whether there is a single goal for the story?

This can be a bit tricky, because sometimes writers stumble into this problem of split goals without consciously intending to do so, thus muddying the waters. If you find that your story is split with multiple goals driving the story, then ask the following question: Are the goals sourcing from the same character, or do the various goals source from different characters.

If your split goals source from one character, then you are working with a central protagonist and you have a team story. If however, you have multiple goals and they are distributed between multiple characters, then you are probably dealing with an ensemble story.

You then have to start looking at some of the other answers from your team questions to see how this all fits together. Juggling your various questions and answers will point your nose to a final answer.

If you determine that you have many goals belonging to several main characters, this is the second big red flag you have an ensemble story.

3. Are there many storylines and none of them stand out as more important than the others?

There are always many storylines in any narrative. The mainline plot drives the overall narrative and this is supported by one or more subplots. This can get confusing when subplots begin to overwhelm the mainline plot, or when they find themselves becoming more interesting than the original plot line you had in mind.

So, the key to clarifying this question lies in properly identifying each subplot, making sure it is playing its proper role in the story. You do this by asking three clarifying questions:

- Does the subplot's POV character reflect the protagonist's moral flaw, or does this POV character have their own distinct moral problem?
- Does the subplot intersect the mainline plot and affect how the mainline story unfolds in the end?
- If you pulled the subplot out of the mainline story, would it hurt or help the telling of the story?

On the first bullet, what I mean by "reflect the protagonist's flaw" is that the subplot POV character needs to have a problem/flaw of their own, absolutely, but that it needs to be a reflection of the protagonist's problem. If the protagonist of the story is grappling with an issue of feeling not good enough (this is their moral blind spot), then the POV subplot character needs to be dealing with this same emotional issue, but from a different perspective. If the subplot represents a different perspective on the protagonist's problem, then it opens a new window into understanding the hero/heroine. This is what a subplot should ideally accomplish in a story. But, the way it does this is by reflecting the protagonist's moral component and thus giving the reader/viewer a new angle on the issue motivating the protagonist in the overall narrative. This is difficult to achieve, and most writers fail miserably at this because they do not fully understand the role of the moral component in a story, nor the proper role a subplot plays in a story. If you find yourself in that boat, I suggest you read my book *Anatomy of a Premise Line* or get the *Rapid Story Development #5: The Moral Premise–How to Build a Bulletproof Narrative Engine for Any Story* e-book.

In the second bullet, what I mean by "intersecting" is that any good subplot should unfold as usual in its separate "story space," but at some strategic point is should fold back around and rejoin the mainline story. The subplot moves along its merry way but does not stay independent. It eventually comes back with a fury, or a whimper, and throws some complication, or new insight, or some new development into the protagonist's situation that then affects how the protagonist acts in their mainline story. Every subplot in a story should have this intersection with the mainline story if the story is a team story (which every story is if it's not an ensemble story). If a subplot does not come back around and intersect the mainline story, then it is truly an independent storyline and stands alone. This is either intentional by the writer (and thus indicates a possible ensemble), or unintentional by the writer and is episodic writing that needs to be fixed.

The last bullet is fairly clear: what would happen if you pulled the subplot out of the story? If things hold up and nothing is affected, then you can be pretty sure that the subplot is independent. But, you also have to ask the next question: why is it in the story if it doesn't do anything? If it is an ensemble story, then its standalone nature is acceptable because it is in service to the bigger thematic message of the bigger story. But, if it is a team story, then an ineffectual subplot will be a pacing problem, at the least, and should be removed or rewritten so that it is a stronger subplot.

If you have determined that there are many storylines and they do not impact the overall effectiveness of the larger narrative, then this is a third big red flag that you have an ensemble story.

Asking these seven questions (four team-related, three ensemble-related) will help you leverage previous information in other chapters, and make this information less academic and more practical. The chances of you not being able to move from this point in your analysis of a story with confidence and a direction are highly remote. But, there may still be some pesky problems that arise, which may undermine your clarity and confidence to move forward—not the lease of which is the issue of mixing forms.

Remember, earlier on I asked the questions, "Should the story be some mix of the two [team vs. ensemble]? Is mixing them even an option?" This is probably the most common scenario that will threaten to derail your efforts for story clarity. Stories that exist in the "gray zone" of partly team, partly ensemble can be crazy making and frustrating. But, as I will lay out in some detail, with examples, in the next chapter, that gray zone will reveal itself to be not so gray after all.

As you apply all the information and analysis you have learned to this point to the examples in the next chapter, you will see that every story, while possibly mixing both team and ensemble characteristics, will always belong more to one form than the other.

THE GRAY ZONE

WHEN ENSEMBLES FEEL LIKE TEAMS AND TEAMS FEEL LIKE ENSEMBLES

A t this point in our examination we have defined teams and ensembles, we have given some characteristic indicators that help refine those definitions, we have examined some "pure" story forms of teams and ensembles, and we have offered a basic strategy for how to decide which story form might best fit a story you are writing, or that could help you figure out which kind of form you have on an already existing story.

But, what do you do if you come across a story that doesn't belong to either the team or ensemble formats (purely)? This is a widespread occurrence, as most writers do not intentionally write team or ensemble stories. They know they will have a large cast of characters, but they do not know there is a process or a methodology that can assist them in the writing. In other words, they are not conscious writers. Not bad or wrong, but the less you know about why you are doing what you do, the more prone you are to finding the quicksand.

TEAM OR ENSEMBLE?

Okay, let's put all this knowledge to the test. Below are examples of stories that straddle the presentation fence. They have both team and ensemble characteristics. Let's apply what we know to see if we can push them over to one side or the other (nature and storytelling hates fence sitters).

The examples that follow are probably stories you have heard of, but many you may have never seen or read. I suppose I could have used examples like *The Simpsons* or *The Hunger Games*, but I think there is value in encouraging you to explore older sources, not in the popular zeitgeist. Seeing that the principles we have been discussing apply across time, through any period of popular culture, is another corroborating factor to demonstrate the validity of team story development.

EXAMPLE #1:

The Boys in the Band (National General Pictures, 1970)

A group of gay friends gather to celebrate one of their birthdays, and feathers fly when an unexpected "straight" friend of the party's host makes a surprise entrance.

Why the confusion? It could be argued that this is just a gathering of individuals, each with their own stories to tell and no real objective at hand. They don't have some common goal, there seem to be several little dramas taking place within the party, and the party itself seems to be the organizing device to bring the men together to create a pressure cooker. But, it's all happening in the same story-time and space, there is a focus on celebrating something, they are all put on the spot by an agonizing "phone game" where they have to call a man they were secretly in love with in the past, and the story closes with a focus on one character as he collapses into despair.

Analysis:

Team—Is there a protagonist?: Yes.

Michael. It's his party, he directs most of the dramatic action, the story ends with him and the sad statement that his life will probably not change. Everything revolves around this character.

Ensemble—Is it hard to decide on one central protagonist? No.

Team—Is there a single story goal?: Yes, kind of.

There is the overall goal of having a birthday party, so it could be argued this is the common goal, but this is a bit amorphous and not very concrete. There is, however, a very concrete and personal goal that Michael has that also helps to give a sense of desire line to the protagonist: he wants to out Allan, the old college buddy who shows up to the party and who is "straight." Michael's plan (the cruel phone game) fails miserably, and only exposes his own pathetic self, but that's the point. The whole play/film is about the pain of being closeted, fears of being alone and lonely, and general human alienation. None of the other characters has a clear goal of their own.

Ensemble—Is it unclear whether there is a single goal for the story? Not really.

Team—Are there stages of development? Yes, kind of.

The group forms, it definitely storms, there are moments when the group norms and seems to be working well and humorously together, but there is no real performing stage unless you count the painful phone game where they all work together to carry out that miserable task. All in all, there is a sense of stages, albeit a fragmented sense.

Ensemble—Are there many storylines and none of them stand out as more important than the others? Not really.

There are several personal stories that unfold. In fact, all of the characters have their issues and sorry lives to discuss. But they all serve the bigger picture and they all reflect the issues facing Michael personally. So they have an ensemble feel in the sense that they serve some bigger picture and not a protagonist specifically, but they do reflect back on the protagonist in a fairly clear way.

Team—Is the mainline story one continuous dramatic narrative? Yes.

The party, Michael's centrality, the building pressures and tension all flow in a continuous dramatic flow to a predictable and unpleasant ending. All the separate dramas feed into this flow and add to it, rather than playing out on the sidelines.

Ensemble—Is the story written episodically with purpose? No.

The story is not episodic, nor are the subplots.

Conclusion: This story falls squarely on the team-story side of the fence. While it has some ensemble sensibilities, the responses to the questions clearly favor team and not ensemble.

EXAMPLE #2:

Contagion (Warner Bros., 2011)

Contagion follows the spread of a deadly virus, MEV1, along with individual stories of people affected, attempts by medical researchers and public health officials to identify and contain the disease, the breakdown of social order in a pandemic, and finally the discovery of a vaccine and the aftermath of the pandemic.

Why the confusion? The goal of the story is clear: stop the disease. Everyone shares this goal or is a reflection of the problem by way of being a victim or survivor. Along the way we follow the stories of victims (Beth and Mitch Emhoff and their children Clark and Jory) who end up dying, one survivor who has an immunity (Mitch), political and social issues play out as some maneuver to leverage the opportunity for profit (conspiracy theorist Alan Krumwiede), while others (CDC doctors Cheever, Haxtall and Mears) leverage powerful social forces to do what has to be done to contain the pandemic.

There are several separate storylines, but they all relate to the main story of the pandemic, but still feel a bit separate. Several characters stand out at different places in the story, but no one person drives the narrative, and yet all the characters are pursuing the same basic goal(s) and struggle to either see it achieved or provide some opposition to thwart its achievement. There is a mix of many team and ensemble characteristics in this story and it would not be hard to see how one could argue either case.

Analysis:

Team—is there a protagonist?: No.

It might be argued that doctor Cheever is the main character and his opponent is the conspiracy blogger Alan Krumwiede, but Mitch also plays a significant role in the story as the grieving survivor trying to save the only family he has left (Jory). But, in the end, while the criminal profiteering plot of Krumwiede plays out against Cheever's attempts to just do his job, and as Mitch and Jory struggle to just get a normal life back, we are left not focused on their subplot. There is no convincing place to put our search for a central protagonist.

Ensemble—Is it hard to decide on one central protagonist? Yes.

No explanation necessary.

Team—Is there a single story goal?: Yes, kind of.

There is clearly the overall goal to find a cure and stop the disease. But, Mitch just wants to find safety for himself and

Jory, and Cheever wants to save his wife and do his job. Other characters have their own goals ranging from profiting off the pandemic (Krumwiede) to finding a cure (Haxtall, others). The goal that seems to override all the individual ones is the curing of the disease, and it dominates the story, much as it would in a team story. But, even so, it is not personal in that sense, it is universal/global.

Ensemble—Is it unclear whether there is a single goal for the story? Not really.

No explanation necessary.

Team—Are there stages of development? Yes, kind of.

The crisis certainly has a forming stage, as any disaster movie or story does when the book or film opens. It is the proverbial calm before the storm and then all hell breaks loose. But this forming is not the forming of some unified team set about a specific task. That happens but only late into the story when the CDC is assigned the job of stopping the crisis, but this team does not include many of the main characters like Mitch or Krumwiede). The story itself spends most of the time in the storming stage (if a stage is recognized at all), and then dwindles down to a twelfth-hour vaccine discovery saving the day. This is hardly a state representing a final performing stage as would be present in a team story. So there are vague impressions of some stages, but nothing convincing that can be definitively identified.

Ensemble—Are there many storylines and none of them stand out as more important than the others? Yes, but one does stand out.

There are clearly separate stories: Mitch and his family, the blogger and his plot, Cheever and his role as leader, Haxtall as researcher on a mission, and while they all have their moments where they stand out, the one that ultimately dominates all others is the general line of the disease itself and stopping it.

Team—Is the mainline story one continuous dramatic narrative? Not really.

This is another difficult question with this story. No one personal storyline of the story stands out as the mainline, but there is still a sense of one continuous narrative because the disease procedural dominates everything. This is not a personal story, but it is a powerful background against which the personal stories play out.

Ensemble—Is the story written episodically with purpose? No.

The story is basically episodic, but not purposefully. The episodic nature of the story is due to the ensemble elements that overshadow the team elements.

Conclusion: This story is extremely difficult to nail down, but given the above analysis it falls more to the ensemble side of the fence. Even saying that I find myself scratching my head and saying, "Hmmm, not so fast." But, I believe this is the right call. *Contagion* is a wonderful example of how very talented and brilliant artists (Stephen Soderbergh and Scott Burns) can get caught in the quicksand and succumb to the consequences. In this case, the consequences were nearly universal reactions to the story being emotionally shallow, procedurally interesting (re the mechanics of a pandemic), but impersonal and detached. If this were a team story with a clear protagonist with personal stakes we could root for, and more of a classic team structure, then I'm convinced this would have had a more dramatically satisfying project.

EXAMPLE #3:

Waiting for Godot (by Samuel Beckett)

Waiting for Godot follows two characters, Vladimir (Didi) and Estragon (Gogo), as they wait for the arrival of a third man named Godot—who never arrives. As they wait, they engage three other characters in the course of discussing a wide range of esoteric topics.

Why the confusion? The play is often referred to as a "small ensemble" play. Because there is nothing going on, in terms of action, the eclectic conversations that result, for most, speak to pure theater and character studies. This is one piece that closely approximates the definition of an ensemble that opens this book. And yet, there is a sense of linearity to the work, the flow moves toward some meeting with a mysterious "other," and both Didi and Gogo appear to share a common goal. There is a clear main-line story (the waiting), and any subplots (Pozzo and Lucky) only unfold in the context of the two men waiting for Godot. The consensus with most is that Waiting for Godot is a traditional ensemble play and has very little in common with traditional storytelling or anything as crass as some subgenre of commercial entertainment.

Analysis:

Team—is there a protagonist?: Yes.

Vladimir (Didi) is the main character. Many critics would fight this assertion, but I believe it is correct. Didi is the one who is most clear about the goal, is directive and continually encouraging of Estrogen (Gogo) to wait with him and postpone ideas of suicide. Didi seems to be in the most pain emotionally and appears to be the most perturbed by Godot's absence. He also appears to the audience as the one through whom we experience most of the dramatic action, consequently, most audiences identify with him, not Gogo.

Ensemble—Is it hard to decide on one central protagonist? Yes.

While there are some indications that Didi fulfills many of the tasks of a protagonist, may not be clear enough for many observers. Ultimately Didi is the one who is the most animated and the most invested in the action, consequently, he can be considered more of a protagonist than not. But, the two men are so symbiotically connected that it is understandable that this could be difficult to see.

Team—Is there a single story goal?: Yes.

The two men are there for one reason, even if Gogo forgets initially why he is there: to meet Godot. The other characters have no interest in this objective, they are truly not on this tangent.

Ensemble—Is it unclear whether there is a single goal for the story? Not really.

No explanation necessary.

Team—Are there stages of development? No.

There are no stages of development. There is only the predicament of writing for someone who never comes, and the tensions that arise from this frustration.

Ensemble—Are there many storylines and none of them stand out as more important than the others? Yes, but one does stand out.

Nothing may happen in this play, from an action perspective, but the point of the play and the line of dramatic flow for the narrative is clear. The line that stands out is the waiting for Godot line. Everything else that happens is in service to this line.

Team—Is the mainline story one continuous dramatic narrative? Yes.

The main characters don't do anything else. They wait. They may talk about many things, but the mainline story stays consistent.

Ensemble—Is the story written episodically with purpose? Yes.

The introductions of Pozzo and Lucky are separate stories that are not so complicated as to pull the audience out of the main Godot line. The subplots (if they can be called that) generate esoteric interest, dramatic interactions, and enhance the mainline story, rather than detract.

Conclusion: Here we have one of the great pieces of world literature, a play that has been analyzed *ad nauseam* by critics, actors, directors, and theoreticians. Many will find applying some brute force methodology like this one to such a delicate work of art to be abhorrent, if not downright criminal. Get over it. Story is story. How stories work and how they are told are not the privileged knowledge of a select, gifted few. This knowledge is the property of no one but is knowable and accessible to everyone. And whether you agree with the parameters and guidelines listed in this book or not, the principles it espouses play out in the crudest limerick or the loftiest piece of theater. Yes, *Waiting for Godot* is a work of genius, but it is also a narrative story, and as such it has no choice but to follow the best practices of good storytelling and narrative design. The genius part, of course, doesn't hurt either.

GRAY ZONE — SPECIAL CASES

The three examples above certainly show the grayness and the sometimes messy quality of identification. In many ways, and this is very much something I love about the lack of exactitude with story development when stories start developing fuzzy bits that crossover, cross-pollinate, and crisscross forms the development becomes so much more fun and challenging. There is no such thing as a story that is equally fifty-fifty team and ensemble, any more than there is any genre that is one-hundred per cent pure genre. All genres bleed into one another to one degree or another. It is this gray zone that is so much fun and helps to stretch us as writers and creators of art (or at least good content).

There are a couple of special cases worth looking at, as we conclude, one that causes confusion and one that causes frustration.

SPECIAL CASE: ANTHOLOGY

Anthologies and ensembles have a lot in common, but they are not the same. Anthologies are collections of things: music, poems, short stories, etc. They are usually presented in some way that demonstrates how all of the pieces fit within the anthology whole. For example a collection of stories all set in one location, or a set of poems all dealing with suicide, or a collection of novellas all dealing with boxing.

As mentioned earlier in this e-book, ensemble stories are also set up with some device or narrative element that connects all the various pieces of the ensemble: theme, idea, physical location, etc. But in ensembles, the connection is deep and meaningful, whereas in an anthology this connection is usually superficial and simplistic. Anthology interconnectedness is a nice way of telling a reader or viewer the anthology pieces belong in the same book or movie, but it doesn't go much deeper than that. Ensemble stories present a much more profound and meaningful interconnection between ensemble story elements.

Some good examples of anthologies are the following:

- *Tales From the Crypt* (HBO, 1989)
- *The Twilight Zone* (CBS, 1959)

- *The Decameron* (United Artists, 1971)
- *New York Stories* (Touchstone Pictures, 1989)
- *Black Mirror* (Channel 4 Television Corp., 2011)
- *Iti, Tomari Dhaka* (Impress Telefilm, 2018)

It should be no surprise many of these are horror or fantasy genres. Often anthologies are collections of stories that satisfy a genre form and so fit together nicely. *New York Stories* and *Iti* are two examples of drama series that are anthologies connected by the love of a city (New York, Dhaka). *The Decameron* is a cinematic rendition of Bocaccio's *Il Decameron* (1370s), an infamous, bawdy, and tragic frame story set in the days of the plague in Florence, Italy. The book follows seven young women and three young men who have fled to the countryside. Each night for two weeks each member of the group trades off telling stories, to pass the time. By the end of the second week, they have told one-hundred stories. *Il Decameron* is very much an ensemble story, not an anthology, as the storytellers know one another, exist in a self-contained world and influence one another by their storytelling. The film *The Decameron*, however, is pure anthology and captures none of the subtlety of the original book. (*It may be significant to note that even with a work as ancient as Il Decameron the ideas and principles presented here apply as clearly as they do to a TV series developed in 2018.*)

The Decameron and *Il Decameron* illustrate perfectly the distinction between an anthology collection and an ensemble story. One is superficial in its sense of interconnectedness, while the other goes deeper to create more connective tissue at the level of characterizations, situations within stories, etc. Even so, it is difficult sometimes for readers or viewers to distinguish between an anthology and an ensemble story. This is mainly due to the fact that they do not fully understand how the two presentations differ.

SPECIAL CASE: THE WORST CASE

I don't give guarantees, they don't exist. But, I can assure you that you will come across this special case. The day will come when you find a story, or devise one, that refuses to cooperate.

The love story where neither lover stands out as central, and there is no goal in the story, but they are playing out a relationship that feels interdependent, but spend a great deal of time living their own lives in separate subplots that don't intersect the love story, and yet the narrative flow feels more unified than episodic. And there are no stages, as such, but if there is one then it would have to be the storming stage because they are fighting all the time and never seem to find a resolution, even in the end. But, the story seems to work.

Or the family drama where because the bridge is washed out and a storm rages, they are all forced the be in one small cabin for one painful night of family tension and squabbling, interspersed with moments of comic relief. There is no specific goal, individual family member pair off with other family members to run separate dramas within the drama, none of which significantly add to the bigger family argument, and no one member seems to stand out as a protagonist or antagonist, yet the setup gives a sense of unified hole and is much more continuous than episodic. And there are suggestions of stages of development, but mostly storming with occasional norming, but they came in already formed and they end the story more dysfunctional than functional, so there is never a point where they perform, as such. And yet, the story still works.

I could easily come up with many other examples of mish-mashes of team and ensemble characteristics in narrative scenarios that readers or viewing audiences would ultimately classify as satisfying. How is that possible? How can a story be a mess from a team/ensemble perspective and still be satisfying? The answer is simple: form is not function (remember chapter one?).

The story is the thing, not the genre or the subset (team/ensemble). Story is what works in the end, that's why you have to learn story development, as well as this material. The genre/forms are narrative tricks writers use to tell a story. Some tricks work better than others based on the story being told, that's why you have to try different things out to see what works best as a narrative vehicle. There are no guarantees the story that fires your imagination and passion will fall neatly into Mr Jeff Lyons's story-form-machine (thank goodness). But, you will never know whether you are on the right track, or any track if you don't know *before* you start writing whether what you are doing is the optimal approach for your story unless you know what you're doing! And you can only know what you're doing by learning the best practices and the mechanics of craft.

If you run into these worst cases, they will only frustrate and infuriate you, if you are unconscious in your development process. But, if you have the tools, techniques, and applications down cold, then you can consciously decide to leave the story alone (because it works as is), or muck around with it to tweak team or ensemble elements to make the story work even better.

CONCLUSION

O n October 1, 1939, Winston Churchill gave a
famous radio address where he attempted to
describe his views regarding the Soviet Union and
its potential role in the unfolding events in the first months of
war in Europe. Of Russia, he said, " I cannot forecast to you the
action of Russia. It is a riddle wrapped in a mystery inside an
enigma, but perhaps there is a key."

The "key" for Churchill to understanding Russia rested in
understanding the nature of national interest. It was not in the
Soviet Union's national interest to allow Germany unfettered
access to the Russian Steps, or easy subjugation of the Slovak
peoples of Southern Europe. The key to the enigma was
knowing what larger picture was being served, beyond the
details of Russian peculiarities.

So, why this historical digression? Simply this: What Churchill understood about Russia is no different than what you can understand about story. The key to the enigma of story lies not in the details of its riddles and mysteries, but in knowing what interest is being served above all else. Even if that interest is purely to entertain, the clarity of knowing that fact is what lights the way to a clear path of development, and success in the writing process.

The central purpose of this e-book, as stated earlier, is to emphasize the team nature of most storytelling, and to arm you with the information and tools necessary for you to not only identify what a story is but how to approach the writing process to deliver the best presentation possible. You are a better writer if you know what you're doing and why you are doing it. You are the writer, so do what you want, but now the claim of ignorance cannot be made and you are accountable for the final results— not to the story police! There is no such thing—no, you are accountable to *you, even more than to the reader*, and that's the good news.

So that your stories do not end up riddles wrapped in mysteries inside enigmas, know your intention, know your plan, know the greater interest being served—and that interest is *always* what is best for the telling of the story, not the presentation of the story. It is the story told by the master craftsperson that is the story that will be remembered.

ADDENDUM 1

TEAM DEVELOPMENT IN THE ACTION-ADVENTURE GENRE

The following example illustrates how the four stages of team development might play out in an action-adventure story in a book series, feature film, or TV series. Notice that the four stages are divided into beats. The number of beats will vary from genre to genre, but the essential idea is that the four stages are always present in any team story. How those stages need to be layered to accommodate particular genre story beats and pacing is what determines the number of "beats" within each stage.

But, don't get caught up in beats vs. stages; the essential concept to take away here is that team development stages are always present in the development of a team-based story, but genre specifics and beat requirements dictate a further refinement of each stage to accommodate genre-specific story beats and pacing, and the number of these refinements (beats) varies from genre to genre.

Later on, I will add additional appendices to this e-book with examples of stage/beat development for other story genres (rom-com, horror, mystery, etc.) to further illustrate team building principles along broader applications.

In the example that follows for the action-adventure genre, the four stages of team development are subdivided into seven total beats. Woven within and without all the team stages are the genre beats each stage must pass through to accommodate the necessary story beats required by the genre. Every genre is made of different beats or story milestones that are character-istic of that genre; every genre is thus different in how it expresses the individual beats/milestones that characterize its genre, but every genre will have the same four stages of team development regardless of any genre-specific beats.

Don't get caught up in the genre beats/milestones versus stages distinctions, I'll deal with genre beats/milestones in a later e-book on how to build genres. Right now, for our purposes, I want you to focus on the concept of team develop-ment stages, because while many writers are well versed in genre beats and genre structures, almost all miss this crucial piece of team story development, regardless of the form of the story they may be developing (novel, feature film, television series, etc.).

FORMING STAGE

Beat 1: (initiating contact) The powers-that-be seek out and hire or force through intimidation a reluctant hero/heroine to do their dirty work and save the day from some monster/threat/predicament.

Beat 2: (actual team forms) The hero/heroine gathers team members (*membership*) or has to manage a rag-tag group already assembled for them to lead. Team *goals* are clarified, *roles* are usually defined here, or emerge over the course of the gathering/recruitment process (we see windows into various characters talents/skills). By the end of this stage, we know what the team's goal(s) is, who the members are, and what roles they will play on the team (plucky comic relief; deadly, vixen, sex kitten; brainiac computer tech; coldblooded assassin, etc.).

STORMING STAGE

Beat 3: (internal team problems) The newly assembled team members distrust one another and posture, challenge, or confront each other for dominance or authority. Internal team alliances start forming, romances form, loyalties start to split, the team fragments. Often, another alpha leader often emerges at this stage. The team is more focused on internal struggles than the external threat they were hired to resolve.

Beat 4: (leadership challenge) The hero/heroine's leadership is usually challenged by the other alpha team member, but the challenge is put down (exacerbating tensions). The reluctant hero/heroine forces a fragile, shaky truce within the team. This is usually the moment the hero/heroine has to finally commit to being a leader. The hero/heroine reorients team to its original purpose and knocks heads if necessary, thus winning respect.

NORMING STAGE

Beat 5—First Team Test: (consensual agreements to cooperate) The opposition/monster/threat makes itself felt by menacing the external world, not the team directly. The team rallies in response to test its shaky alliance. The team is not seasoned, and previous dysfunctions reveal weaknesses in team effectiveness. The team gets beaten up, and it's humiliating. The opponent is now fully aware of the team's presence, but is unimpressed, and bent on destroying them. The powers-that-be question the wisdom of their decision to bring in the hero/heroine.

Beat 6—Second Team Test: (new suggestions for team effectiveness) The team's ego is bruised so they brainstorm how to fix themselves. First signs of cohesion and real cooperation. The hero/heroine steps up training, dysfunction peaks. The team starts to revisit the storming stage again. The hero/heroine's leadership is seriously challenged by the other alpha member, or rather than challenge leadership they decide to betray the team and form an alliance with the opponent—setting the team up for defeat. The opponent raises the stakes again to draw the team out in order to destroy it. This is where the first major team death occurs, or major injuries. At this point, the hero/heroine is often disenfranchised, or isolated, or fired by the powers-that-be. The team is often at its wits-end and rudderless.

PERFORMING STAGE

Beat 7—Third Team Test: The team is shaken by events, but

puts aside differences, rallies behind the hero/heroine, and creates new resolve to do what they were hired to do. Talents rise, cohesion increases, the hero/heroine is reinstated, or reinstates him-herself against the will of the powers-that-be. The team is now at peak performance and they take on the enemy to victory. In some stories this is where most of the team dies, leaving the hero/heroine standing with one or two others as the only survivors. But, in many book and TV series, the team is left intact so that sequels or new episodes can be written—because nothing kills a series faster than killing off characters readers or audiences have grown to love.

SUMMARY

This genre-specific example is one example of how genre beats play out within the context of team stages of development. Within any genre, you will find that all the story beats that make a genre a genre will unfold fairly neatly within all the four stages. And even if you find it difficult in a team story you are developing to clearly identify where specific genre beats need to go, if you keep thinking "function" and work on figuring out how any genre beat might relate to forming, storming, norming, or performing chances are you will start to see the logical placement of any genre beat in your team structure.

If for some reason, you can't see where a beat belongs, don't stress it. Just put it wherever you think it belongs and you will be fine. It's better to have the guidelines and end up with a few outliers than it is to have no guidelines and end up with nothing but outliers. Over time, I will add future appendices of other genres to further demonstrate how the beats and stages play out in other genres (love story, horror, etc.).

ADDENDUM 2

TEAM DEVELOPMENT IN THE ROMANCE GENRE

The romance genre is a fascinating genre in creative writing. More than any other genre form (except perhaps science fiction) it has evolved into a well-established complex of subgenres and marketing categories with clearly identified story elements, beats, and flow. As of this writing, it is the most popular and lucrative genre for writers today. What's more, romance publishers give romance writers tremendous support in developing their stories, be that in the form of detailed author guidelines for subgenre requirements, strong editorial support for imprint content development, and an ever-growing list of subgenre and category areas allowing for authors to spread their wings and try new categories and formats, and the list goes on.

In addition, when you consider that romance can mix with many other genres to create subgenres (romance paranormal, romance mystery, romance action-adventure), the complexity and depth of development possibilities can be staggering. Granted, most genre fiction today is mixed-genre, but romance is particularly situated to leverage cross-genre pollination for success.

When it comes to the love/romance genres, there are many story gurus who have created templates for genres story beats. It should be noted that love stories and romance stories are not the same things. All romance stories include a love story component, but not all love stories contain a romance. Romance stories focus on the falling-in-love process, and the coming together of two people who refuse to admit they belong together (with varying degrees of dysfunction, eroticism, or/or emotional dithering).

As I said, there are many story development experts who have come up with their own proprietary story beats for romantic comedies, love stories, etc., and when you review the literature you realize that they are all describing many of the same basic genre beats, regardless of the proprietary names they may give their structure steps.

The following example of team development in the romance genre is based on the work of Gwen Hayes. I highly recommend you check out her work listed in the "Acknowledgments" section. I have selected her approach to the romance structure because I think she has done the best job pulling together the pure genre-story requirements while incorporating the best of pre-existing genre models currently in the literature. I know many members of the Romance Writers of America (RWA), the premier organization for romance writers, who follow Gwen's model (though the RWA does not endorse any particular structure approach), consequently, I believe it will be instructive to use this model for our analysis.

What I find striking about Gwen's take on the romance genre is that she intuitively divided her structure for romance into four parts: setup, falling love, retreating from love, and fighting for love. She called them different things, but functionally these parts perfectly correspond to the four stages of team development. This is another corroborating indicator, for me, that team stages are natural to storytelling and not only "some guy's" invention. There is a reason Ms Hayes did what she did: her natural story sense took her down the right river, rather than into the floodplain, because her intuition about story structure tapped into the principles we have been discussing throughout this e-book.

FORMING STAGE (SET UP)

<u>Beat 1/2</u>: (h1/h2) These are two beats, often separate scenes, that introduce the heroine/hero (remember this is romance, so the protagonists are most often female/male—but not always—same-sex stories are very popular). In keeping with sound story structure principles, this introduction should be visually interesting and revealing of each character's inner angst. This is the team forming stage, so they are not together yet—they haven't met—but the reader is already getting the message they are peas in a pod, they just don't know it yet.

<u>Beat 3</u>: (meet cute) This is the actual meeting of the eventual

lovers. Typically, this is structurally the inciting incident, as it kickstarts the connection and also the external adventure. Still forming the team, the two central characters might be engaged (not literally), but the connection and need for the other is not set in emotional stone.

Beat 4: (no way 1) In keeping with the forming stage, this beat throws the first emotional monkey wrench into the mix. The lovers soon realize this isn't going to happen, nor should it, despite any physical attraction or primal urges. This is an emotional pushback that pushes for quite a while in the story, and it begins in the forming stage.

Beat 5: (adhesion plot thrust) Just when the lovers think that they might not be locked into anything, they get locked. Something happens that forces them to be reliant on one other, or dependent, or literally connected at the hip. Many devices can be used to accomplish this, but the idea is they are in it together now, for better or worse, and there's nothing they can do about it. The team is now formed.

NORMING STAGE (FALLING IN LOVE)

Beat 6: (no way 2) Now that the team is formed, the first internal problems begin to emerge, but it has not broken out into full-on storming. One or both of the lovers dig in their heels on the original "no way" belief as a way of defending themselves from the forced unity they now suffer.

Beat 7: (inkling this could work) One or both of the lovers blinks, and the armor cracks. We see the beginnings of consideration, "Hmm, maybe ...." This is the beginning of the norming stage where the hint of a common ground emerges, even if not fully realized.

Beat 8: (deepening desire) But, the norming is unavoidable, as *consensual working agreements*, commonalities, irresistible qualities, etc. deepen the connection and the falling in love is in full, or at least undeniable, bloom.

Beat 9: (maybe this will work) This is usually where they have sex, or if not sex then real intimacy (though not happily ever after intimacy). This is clearly the continued evolution of the norming of the relationship with real feelings of "hey, this just might ...."

Beat 10: (midpoint of love plot) The culmination of all the norming, the middle of the development. But, as with any story's midpoint (following story structure best practices), it is the calm before the storm and things are about to ratchet up for the action line as well as for the relationship.

STORMING STAGE (RETREATING FROM LOVE)

Beat 11: (inkling of doubt) Just when the light begins to gather, the cloud passes overhead. The old "no way" nag pops back up, or some new reveal upsets the previous norming culmination. As with any storming stage, the disagreements start, the opposition is sharpened, the rivalries emerge, or any host of possible wrinkles appear that cast doubt on all that has developed.

Beat 12: (deepening doubt) And it only gets worse. The connection is still there, more voluntary than forced, but when all the lovemaking is done, the worries rise up and the doubt is undeniable.

Beat 13: (retreat) The storming may be noisy or quiet (internalized), but the pressures mount and one or both of the lovers bail in whatever way feels right based on the scenario. The bail may be literal, or quietly emotional, but it is an act of self-protection.

Beat 14: (shields up) This is the first confirmation that either of their darkest fears about love is true. The thing they feared might happen (the reason they felt "no way" one or two) is now staring them in the face. The storming stage has come to the breaking point, literally.

Beat 15: (break up) In normal structure this is the first phase of the doom moment, or black moment, or visit to death, or whatever story guru terminology you want to use. All is lost, or at least the other lover is lost, regardless of what action line might be playing out around both protagonists. Ideally, not only do they pull apart due to their own constricting emotional dynamic, but the bad guys, or the ghost, or the serial killer has also made their move and both lovers are coming up short on that plot line as well. All is indeed lost.

PERFORMING STAGE (FIGHTING FOR LOVE)

Beat 16: (dark night of the soul) We begin the performing stage of the drama with an emotional regrouping. In classic structure we are still in the doom moment, but it is the phase where the fall from grace is followed by the realization that even though they might still be deep in their personal flaw, they start to realize that they can't keep operating from this same place—if they do, they will lose everything. They are not changing, but they are entertaining the idea. Consequently, they must snap out of it somehow, regroup and try again, but differently this time. They don't know what that means yet, but that knowledge is coming. This is still the performing stage because it is about changing outcomes; delivering on promises; and moving forward, not backward.

Beat 17: (wake-up/catharsis) This is where the performing stage shows itself: the choice is made to love instead of fear. The character may not fully heal their moral blind spot, but the central choice is made that opens up all possibility for change and resolution. This is the first step to high performance.

Beat 18: (grand gesture) The next step in high performance is acting on the change. Remember, in any story any change in a character must be shown on the page in behavior to have any meaning. You can't have someone contemplating their navel smuggle proud of their inner growth. They have to act on it and show the reader in action how they've changed. This is that moment, and it required high performance in every sense of the words.

Beat 19: (what wholehearted looks like) The lovers are complete, they have taken on the external opposition, not only to their love affair but whoever is threatening the community. They are a team, performing at it's highest level and they are aligned in life and in love. All that's left now is to show the happily-ever-after.

Beat 20: (epilogue) All is well, and it's time to leave, but here is where you want to show how well-matched the lovers are and go out on a nice bit of character business that shows how all too human they are or wrap a nice bow on it (but not too perfect a bow).

(Structure beats based on *Romancing the Beat: Story Structure for Romance Novels*, by Gwen Hayes, 2016)

SUMMARY

As with the previous appendix, this example falls right into line with the principles of team-based story development. The particular structure we've just looked at is unique in that its creator had the story instincts to group her beats into functionally appropriate categories that, by no conscious mechanism other than her talent, neatly fall into all four stages of team development.

This is not an accident or a fluke. Every genre will "cooperate" in this way. It has no choice because teams are a part of story-telling. Not every story is a team-based story, but most are. We've covered the main area that does not conform to team principles (ensembles), but even there the best practices for that particular subset dictate how you can properly navigate to deliver the desired story. The point is that rather than guessing or crossing your fingers and toes, hoping you get it right, you will have the basic knowledge to be able to test, validate, and choose which subset (teams or ensembles) best applies to the story you want to tell.

PART V

RAPID STORY DEVELOPMENT #5: THE MORAL PREMISE—HOW TO BUILD A BULLETPROOF NARRATIVE ENGINE FOR ANY STORY

STORIES VS. SITUATIONS

This is an e-book about stories and moral components. The relationship of one to the other is so critical to the function of storytelling that I realized in writing this e-book that readers would be derailed in the discussion, early on, if I did not create a solid basis for understanding why a moral premise and a story are connected at the proverbial hip, indeed are essential to one another in the telling of any story. A writer cannot be expected to fully grasp the importance of a moral premise if he or she does not fully understand the nature of a story and how "stories" are not all created equal when it comes to moral elements.

So, to that end this opening chapter will tackle the important topics of what a story is, what a story is not, why this distinction is important to you as a writer, and how you can proceed when you are sure you have a story—or whatever it is you have if you don't have a story (yes, there is a name for it, but hang in there).

WHAT IS A STORY?

"Story" is a common *term'd art* in the world of creative writing —everyone knows what a story is, right? You would think so, but, alas, this is not the case. So don't be offended by my question, because what we're about to discuss is something that is not taught in writing classes, MFA programs, or written about in most writing-craft, how-to books. Knowing how to tell that you have a story and that it can survive the long story development process from beginning to end, is not some random bit of knowledge you pick up off the grass. It is skill that can be learned, like riding a bike and once learned, it can lift your storytelling craft to a level of mastery that will save you time, money and months of frustration writing yourself into literary corners and blind alleys.

To appreciate the power of what I am about to describe, we must first begin with two obvious questions: what do I mean when I use the term "a story," and if something is not a story, then what is that something else?

When I ask groups of writers (novelists or screenwriters) to define this most basic storytelling idea, "what is a story?" I get as many definitions as there are people in the room. The responses are always generic and canned:

- A story is a narrative.
- A story is the sequential beats of what happens in a story.

- A story is your plot.
- A story is what your characters do.
- A story is a narration of events coming to some conclusion.

All of these (and there are many others) have some ring of truth to them and for the most part, suffice when it comes to answering the question "what is a story?," but none of these definitions defines the thing itself in a way that has meaning and significance for storytellers. So, here is a working definition of a story that captures the essence of the thing:

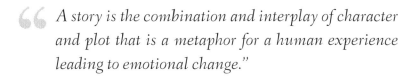 *A story is the combination and interplay of character and plot that is a metaphor for a human experience leading to emotional change."*

Essentially, what this is saying is that if you are writing something that involves an individual carrying out actions on the page that combine to create a personal experience of emotional change and that experience conveys some insight into the human condition, then you have a story. Given this definition, it then follows that a story possesses five identifiable components:

THE FIVE COMPONENTS OF A STORY:

- A story reveals something about the human condition or makes a statement about what it means to be human.

- A story tests personal character, over and over, to reveal deeper character.
- A story has subplots that are dramatic and thematic reflections of the journey of the protagonist, and that opens windows into character and motivation.
- A story ends in a different emotional space then it began.
- A story is driven by a strong moral component motivating the protagonist through the middle of the story, resulting in dramatically interconnected scene writing.

This list of bullets is not arbitrary or pulled out of some hat like a rabbit by a magician. No, these components derive from story structure itself, that's why they are real and possess the full force of drama (or comedy). Every story has a structure. If it doesn't, then it's not a story, it's something else.

If you have these five components clearly identified in your writing, then you can have confidence you have a story, and not that something else. You can be confident that there is an underlying foundation supporting any writing that will emerge, and that it will support your entire writing process. It is beyond the scope of this e-book to deal with the topic of story structure and its critical role in the story development process (see my book *Anatomy of a Premise Line: How to Master Premise and Story Development for Writing Success* (Focal Press)), but knowing how to identify a story—before you start writing—is invaluable to novelists struggling with any new story idea, or an old idea that is going nowhere.

This is the craft skill I alluded to earlier. This is that bit of story wisdom that for some comes automatically, elegantly, without thought—as talent—but that for the rest of us comes as learned craft. Regardless of how it comes, as a gift from the gods, or as hard-earned mastery, this knowledge can make all the difference between getting lost in the story woods and writing reams of meandering pages, versus staying focused, directed and intentional in your writing.

What do you do, however, when you write a story only to discover that those five story components are weak, or missing? You love your idea, but don't want to abandon it. This is the other side of this story vs no-story coin. Remember, all stories have a structure. If they don't, then they're not stories, they're something else—that something else is a called a situation.

A situation is what most genre writers (horror, police procedural, detective, mystery, romance, etc.) are creating when they think they are writing stories. Situations are parts of stories, they are not stories themselves, but, they can still be compelling, fun, entertaining and wonderfully engaging. How can you tell if you have a situation? Like stories, situations have five identifiable components.

THE FIVE COMPONENTS OF A SITUATION:

- A situation is a problem, puzzle, or predicament with an obvious and direct solution.

- A situation does not reveal character; it mainly tests a character's problem-solving skills.
- A situation's plot twists ratchet up the puzzle or mystery (stakes), but rarely open character windows.
- A situation begins and ends in the same emotional space, especially for the protagonist.
- A situation has no, or a very weak, moral component, often leading to episodic writing.

The last point (a weak or nonexistent moral component) is the key concept to be aware of. It is, in fact, the single most important element in what constitutes a story vs a situation, and is thus the crown jewel of any real story.

A situation is all about the puzzle, mystery, or problem to be solved. Look at any police procedural TV show, or mystery novel (Agatha Christie, Sherlock Homes, etc.), or most monster movies; they are all about one question: how quickly and cleverly can the protagonist get out of the pickle they are in and solve the problem?

Let's take a classic (and my favorite) set-up: the twenty-something kids caught in a cabin in the woods with the monster/slasher/alien outside trying to get in to eat/slash/probe them. The only questions are: how many kids are going to be eaten/killed/probed, how bloody is it going to get and who will survive? That's it. None of the characters is going to have a big revelatory moment where they realize they have to change their life to be a better person.

There will be no moments where we get profound insights into the inner workings of the protagonist (assuming there is a main character). Any twists or plot complications will be all about ratcheting up the tension of the problem/puzzle, not pushing characters to some behavioral edge where we see who they are as people. The only change in the emotional space will be one of moving from happy-go-lucky (opening), to terror-filled (middle), to relief at surviving (end). In other words, the hero or heroine will end the adventure in the same emotional place inside themselves as they started.

The most important differentiator of all is that there is no, or a very weak, moral component to the situation. A moral component means that any protagonist is driven from the inside by some basic belief about him or herself, which is essentially wrong, but that is coloring all their actions outside themselves in the story world. They are acting badly, because of this characterological blind spot and this is what they heal and change in the end. Every story has this; every situation does not. This one element alone is enough to help you quickly identify a situation from a story. Does your protagonist have a flaw that is screwing up their lives, that they would have anyway, regardless of the threat of being eaten/killed/probed? If the answer is yes, then you have a story and not a situation.

There is, however, one gray-area worth mentioning. This is what I call the "basically good person caught in the no-win scenario" scenario. In the film world, some good examples of this are *Gravity* (2013, Warner Bros.), *The Martian* (2015, Twentieth Century Fox), *Taken* (2008, EuropaCorp.), *Godzilla* (2014, Warner Bros.)—there are many others. These are all situations masquerading as stories, but they fall into this gray area; a little bit story, a little bit (or mostly) situation.

The differentiator that pushes them over the story line into a situation is that the heroes and heroines in all these "stories" are all focused on surviving the problem/disaster/predicament they are facing, not working out some deep-seated flaw that is mucking up everyone's lives around them. They are basically good people, thrust by circumstance (not of their own making) into fighting a losing battle, even though they may win in the end and this is what saves the story day; we root for them because they are getting crushed and find the will to live, or make some horrible choice that saves others. They don't change, they've always been good (no full stop) and they end the story the same way, beat up and a bit worse for the wear—but alive.

All of these movies were *huge* at the box office; great successes financially and with audiences. The fact is, movie/TV audiences love situations and readers love them in fiction. The caveat here is that to be successful on the screen, or in print, situations must overcome their story weaknesses, and this means doing three things: be fun, be entertaining and be engaging.

They may not have anything to say about the human condition, and the protagonist may be a leaf on the wind of fate, motivated only by a will to live and not by some twisted moral flaw they have to overcome in the end, but that's alright as long as the audience has fun, is engaged and is entertained. Stories have to do these three things as well, but stories have the advantage of having a compelling human story driving the drama or comedy, on top of being fun, entertaining and engaging.

However, if you have a situation and you don't want to let it go, then your responsibility as a writer is to make it the best situation you can, from a reader-engagement perspective. Stories are not better than situations, they are more complex. So, write stories that will bring readers to tears, or bust their guts laughing and teach them what it means to be human along the way; or write a situation that will make them bite off their nails and scream out loud in excitement, unwilling to stop reading for fear of missing what's next. Whichever you choose, do it consciously, *be a conscious writer* (see "Appendix 1").

SO, I'M WRITING A STORY

Now that you understand the difference between a story and a situation, if you choose to write a story you now also know that you must have a strong moral component. What does this mean? How do you find one, if you don't have a clue where it might be? And once found, what do you do with it? Answering these questions, and more, is the purpose of the remainder of this e-book.

THE MORAL PREMISE

> 66 *The moral basis of a story will make or break any story—every story needs a strong moral component."*

Screenwriting gurus, script doctors, creative writing teachers, and successful writers in film, TV, and prose fiction have all written about the moral aspect of storytelling. They all tell you, "You need a protagonist who is flawed," or "Your characters have to be broken in some way," or "Your hero/heroine has to be damaged goods."

The idea, of course, is that the more damaged the goods, the more vulnerable and sympathetic they will be, and with something broken, there is something to fix. Even with characters who are evil to the core, like Hannibal Lechter (*Silence of the Lambs*), or Michael Corleone (*The Godfather Trilogy*) their evil has an unconscious quality to it that makes them likable beasts—

they are oblivious to their madness and this gives them the patina of innocence.

Entire books have been written about the moral underpinnings of storytelling and the need to have a moral heart to your story expressed through theme, or some moral argument sewn throughout your story. So, the idea of a moral premise is nothing new, and for many, it may be a tired and overplayed subject that has been adequately written about.

I disagree, not so much because what has previously been written about the topic has been wanting or lacking substance, quite the contrary. There is a lot of great writing and teaching available on the subject of moral storytelling. What is lacking is not the expression of the need to do it in stories, what is lacking is a clear demonstration of how to execute it on the page and in a piece of writing. Very few teachers and commentators articulate a clear strategy for creating characters with convincing and sustainable moral components.

Mostly what you will get are the protagonists straight out of central casting: the self-pitied, alcoholic lawyer crying in his beer because no one believes in him anymore; or the lonely, embittered, hired assassin questioning the meaninglessness of life; or the neurotic, obsessive-compulsive, plucky comic relief who is the sad-clown under all the affected happiness.

All of these tropes are tropes for a reason, they are the easy road, or as they say in business, they are the low hanging fruit. Why climb the tree and risk falling when the effortless sweets are hanging right there in front of you? The reason you want to climb the tree is that you see more from the top and the light is much better to see what you're grabbing. There is more risk, but no one ever wrote anything great playing it safe.

WHAT DOES "MORAL" MEAN?

In my story development workshops, I like to ask a simple question before I start, "What is a story." You would think that in a room full of writers and storytellers that this is a no-brainer question. But, when I go around the room getting answers, the problem quickly emerges: there are as many definitions of a story as there are people in the room. How can that be? How is it possible not to have a consensus or common ground for one of the most basic concepts in creative writing? The answer is that it is not taught (or ineffectually taught). The idea, construct, and utility of this thing called a story is assumed to be known. Everyone knows what a story is, right? So, the gurus, teachers, and experts sally forth and teach their courses without ever establishing a common language and conceptual foundation to guide the teaching process.

It is the same thing with the concept of "moral." But, if you were to do the same thing with this word as I do with the word "story," you would have the same experience. There would be as many definitions for moral as there are people in the room. And yet, everyone has an intuitive understanding of moral, just as they do of story. What they (and we as a community) lack is that common ground and conceptual foundation that establishes an intellectual and creative context for further discussion.

And because this foundation is missing, writers fall back on what they know, or think they know, to answer the question, "What does moral mean?" Most often people will fall back on the easy tropes: the down and out alcoholic, the drug addict, the cheating husband, the bank robber, the pushy lawyer. None of these are moral problems; none of these are moral flaws. But, writers have been taught that these kinds of tropes are the required moral problems every protagonist should have. And herein lies the problem: writers settle for these easy answers. They never ask the next question: why? Why is my protagonist alcoholic? Why is my protagonist robbing banks? Why is my protagonist a jerk?

And so we come to the essence of why this e-book is so important. It will not only define what moral means, but it will show you how to find the right moral flaw for any protagonist. It will show you the more profound questions to ask, how to ask them, and how to apply the results of the asking to your story. Rather than tell you to come up with a great moral problem for your protagonist, this e-book will show you how to build one.

But, before the building must come the foundation. This means coming up with a workable definition that moral philosophers may not like, but that writers will find productive and powerful for their writing.

"MORAL" DEFINITION FOR WRITERS:

66 *'Moral' refers to the principles, behaviors, and*

conduct that specify a person's sense of right and wrong in themselves, and in the world, and that defines their impact in the world as a human being.

We end on this definition because what comes next is a systematic breakdown of why this particular definition works best for creative writers and storytellers. It is worded in a particular way to cover three key areas of any moral premise: motivation, action, and dramatic tension.

In the next chapters we will look at all the pieces you need to construct a powerful moral component, and then show you how to execute it (how deep to go) in your screenplay or novel to maximum effect so that every story you write will resonate with audience appeal, be populated by three-dimensional characters, and possess emotion-based storylines that will be dramatically bulletproof.

WHAT IS A MORAL COMPONENT?

The previous chapter offered a working definition of moral that relates specifically to the function of telling a story. As part of that definition, I stated that three elements were specifically being identified in that definition: behavior, action, and dramatic tension.

Beyond this definition, I would suggest that there is an actual construct that can help you identify, develop, and deliver a powerful moral premise for any story. This construct I call the *moral component*. The term "component" refers to a particular part of some larger whole; a part that contributes to the function of that whole, and to its efficiency. The moral premise, like any complex piece of machinery, is not a single widget working in isolation, but instead made up of many widgets working in harmony to achieve a sole purpose: tell a story.

The moral component of any story is not a single quality or trait you strive to achieve in your novel or screenplay. The moral component is an amalgam of three core elements that work together to achieve the kind of storytelling that lifts any story from the mundane to the memorable. The three elements of any story's moral component consist of the following:

- The moral blind spot
- The immoral effect
- The dynamic moral tension

Moral Blind Spot

The moral blind spot is literally that, a blind spot in the protagonist's sense of right and wrong, not only within themselves, but in the world. The blind spot is a core belief that the protagonist holds that twists their moral compass in such a way as to poison all external relationships. This *core belief* is generated by a *base fear* about themselves, a fear to which they are blind but that nonetheless colors all their *choices, decisions, attitudes, and actions*—all of which results in the hurting of other people, not just themselves. The main character knows their core belief (superficially), is blind to their base fear, and is in denial about the negative impact he/she is having on others.

Characters act out of motivation, and their actions are consistent with those motivations. The moral blind spot is the fuel of character motivation, so any actions a character carries out must be consistent with those motivations. They take on a moral tone because the character choices, decisions, attitudes, and actions negatively affect other people. It's not only inner torment and angst directed against the self (though this could be going on as well). Their behavior emotionally hurts others.

The moral blind spot is about how the protagonist is acting deficiently in the world, harming others, all because they hold a false belief about the world, a belief that throws them into fear (equally wrong) and that then acts as the driver for all scene-level motivation.

Motivation is not about wanting something—motivation is the thing that makes the wanting exist at all. Characters have desire to find tangible objects that can feed the motivation driving their need to want whatever it is they want. Motivation sources from the inside out, not the outside in—it comes from the heart and soul of the character and everything in the story is at service to this inner driver.

The key to understanding here is that this driver while sourcing from the inside, is never purely interior to the character. It must find its physical expression outside the character in the form of scene-level action on the page. This idea is at the heart of the old motto and cliché "show don't tell." The act of showing in a story is not only about making scenes visual; it is about tangibly externalizing, on the page, the internal drive that is wreaking havoc with the protagonist's moral compass (i.e., the blind spot).

Immoral Effect

The immoral effect is the moral blind spot in action; it is how you "show, don't tell." There is no point in having your protagonist suffer from a skewed moral compass unless that skew demonstrates itself in action at the scene level in the novel or screenplay. If your protagonist is hurting other people, then the audience needs to see it happen, not merely know intellectually about the moral blind spot. To reiterate: your protagonist has a base fear that feeds a distorted belief about the world that, in turn, produces actions consistent with that fear and belief.

An excellent example of this is Joe, the bank robber. Joe has a core fear that he is fatally broken and flawed and he'll never figure out what's wrong with him on his own (moral blind spot). So he develops a sense of entitlement (skewed belief), "The world owes me an answer to my problem. Somebody 'out there' has to fix me." In a sense, Joe is waiting for the cavalry to come over the hill to rescue him, but in the meantime, he develops a twisted perception and belief that he's owed something because of he is "the exception," he's the broken one. His core fear is that he is unfixable, his distorted belief is that this makes him entitled, and the immoral effect is that he forcibly takes what is owed him and screw the consequences.

Joe has a blind spot of feeling unfixable and flawed, which he slathers over with a sense of entitlement to assuage the emotional pain of being hopelessly broken. He is unaware of his fear and core belief about himself; all he knows is how he compensates for it (entitlement), and this directs his actions in the world ("I'll take what I want").

Most writers would settle for Joe being a bad guy and robbing banks. So, he's a guy who has to learn how not to be a bad guy. He has to learn not to be greedy and selfish. Or in the parlance of the standard story guru world, he has to figure out his want (money) and his need (to not be selfish/greedy).

The above need/want model is nowhere near what he needs to learn and is not even in the ballpark in clarifying or establishing this character's real moral problem. But, using the cookie-cutter approaches of most story gurus, this is what most writers think is the direction to take Joe as a character. It should be obvious, even with this introductory discussion of Joe, that the blind spot/immoral effect components already deepen his character and will lead to a much more personal and satisfying conclusion for his growth arc in the story.

Dynamic Moral Tension

While the moral blind spot is the driver that generates the immoral effect, the dynamic moral tension is the engine that keeps it all running. Throughout your story, your protagonist will have to make choices, serious choices. He or she will not be choosing vanilla or chocolate, or pizza with or without pepperoni. No, the choices will be: do I cheat on my wife or not, do I kill this person or not, do I rob the bank or not, do I save myself or the infant baby on the train tracks?

The choices are moral, in the context we have established with our definition of a moral premise. And the choices stem from the other two elements of the moral component we have covered, i.e., moral blind spot and immoral effect. Character choice does not exist in a vacuum, it is generated by the engine of the dynamic moral tension that is constantly testing, and prodding, and challenging your protagonist to change and grow, or disintegrate and spiral into a worse moral condition.

This is critical to understand, because the dynamic moral tension, or the lack thereof, is what gives you a passive or active main character in your screenplay or novel. You want your hero or heroine to be active, not passive. What is the difference between the two? An active character is one that generates scene-level action based on the moral component. The active protagonist causes, directly or indirectly, everything that happens in your story. The passive protagonist is the main character that generates nothing, but who is always in reaction-mode responding to external events that force him-her to act. Passive main characters tend to be dull and boring because they get pushed around by events, rather than create the events of the story themselves.

FOUR EXAMPLES:

Before we end this chapter, let's consider four examples from literature, theater, and film that illustrate this blind spot/immoral effect and dynamic moral tension inter-relationship to see how they play out in well-known stories:

Example #1:

Sunset Boulevard (screenplay Billy Wilder, 1950)

Protagonist: Joe Gillis (William Holden)

Moral Blind Spot: Joe feels he has no real value.

Immoral Effect: Joe uses people for advancement, even as he demeans himself; manipulates others to look good.

Blind Spot-Immoral Effect Connection: Because Joe's lack of self-worth haunts him, he seeks out situations that remind him how "less than" he is, despite his hunger for achievement and the need to be admired. It is his ironic lack of value that drives his lust for being valued by others.

Dynamic Moral Tension: Joe is continually being offered the choice to honor himself and leave this dysfunctional relationship and go with the younger woman, or stay and play out his old pattern. He keeps making the bad choice, to his doom.

Example #2:

Amadeus (play Peter Shaffer, 1980; screenplay Peter Shaffer, 1984)

Protagonist: Antonio Salieri (F. Murray Abraham)

Moral Blind Spot: Salieri feels he lacks talent, real genius—he's ordinary.

Immoral Effect: Salieri cannot tolerate anyone excelling at his expense, so he must destroy them.

Blind Spot-Immoral Effect Connection: Because Salieri is driven by a core fear he is mediocre (i.e., ordinary), when faced with real genius in the form of Mozart he obsessively drives Mozart toward his ideal of perfection—and Mozart's doom.

Dynamic Moral Tension: Salieri is continually being offered the opportunity to treat Mozart as a more-talented colleague and be supportive, or continue his plan of manipulation and self-centeredness. He constantly chooses to act in his self-interest.

Example #3:

Of Mice and Men (novel John Steinbeck, 1937; screenplay Horton Foot and John Steinbeck, 1992)

Protagonist: George Milton

Moral Blind Spot: George fears will obliterate him if he lets down his guard.

Immoral Effect: He must compulsively protect Lennie from the world, or else it may destroy him—Lennie being a metaphor for himself.

Blind Spot-Immoral Effect Connection: Even while he resents his role as protector, he so thoroughly identifies with Lennie's vulnerability to the world at large that he dooms both of them to a tragic end, when he is forced by his fear of the world to "protect" Lennie in an ultimate way: taking Lennie out of the world that threatens to destroy them both.

Dynamic Moral Tension: George consistently faces the opportunity to face his fear of the world and let Lennie experience his relationship with life, or maintain his obsessive control, and keeps making the bad choice leading to the worst possible outcome.

Example #4:

The Verdict (novel Barry Reed, 1980; screenplay David Mamet, 1982)

Protagonist: Frank Galvin

Moral Blind Spot: Frank is blind to the fact that he sees himself as valueless and not mattering.

Immoral Effect: He sees people as targets and easy prey for money; people don't matter, they're a means to an end.

Blind Spot-Immoral Effect Connection: Frank takes advantage of people because they have no value to him, beyond what he can manipulate out of them, but he feels this about other people because he has no sense of worth about himself. He would not hurt other people if he found himself valuable; which is exactly what he does by the end of the story, reclaiming his humanity.

Dynamic Moral Tension: Frank is offered multiple opportunities to do the right thing because it's the right thing, rather than going for the easy money and the selfish payout, ultimately realizing he has dignity and value as a human being and that's worth fighting for.

All of these examples show the subtle and complex relationships between the three elements of the moral component. This single construct is the engine of any story's middle; it is the thing that drives the narrative forward and helps the writer raise dramatic stakes and throw a story's protagonist into ever deeper and dangerous emotional waters. The proactive vs passive nature of a protagonist is what makes or breaks the middle of any story. And how active or reactive a protagonist depends on how well these three elements play together.

To more clearly see this dynamic relationship, it will be helpful to examine how it plays out graphically in the "Active Protagonist Loop" and the "Passive Protagonist Loop" detailed in the next chapter. These illustrations show clearly why the moral component acts as the main line of demarcation between any story and situation.

ACTIVE VS PASSIVE PROTAGONISTS

I n the previous chapter, I introduced the concepts of passive and active protagonists and the moral component dynamics that contributed to a proactive vs reactive main character. All that was theoretically interesting, but a picture is worth a thousand words, so in this chapter we will look at how the three elements of the moral component (moral blind spot, immoral effect, dynamic moral tension) work inside a story to deliver the most robust possible narrative engine for dramatic or comedic action.

THE PASSIVE PROTAGONIST LOOP:

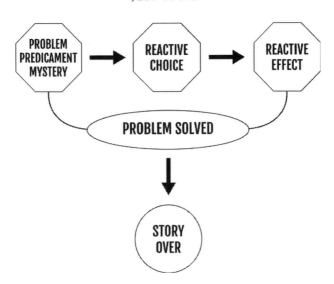

As I explained in the first chapter on stories vs situations, in a narrative with a passive protagonist, the hero-heroine face a problem-mystery-predicament. They did not create the problem themselves, the problem finds them, and they have to decide how to act. Their response to the problem, however, is reactive, not proactive. The situation is leading them; they are not leading the situation. Situations (and not stories) tend to have passive protagonists for this very reason. The situation drives the hero-heroine in situations, not the other way around. The passive protagonist is forced by events to make a reactive choice, which then leads to a reactive effect (their choice in action).

The bottom part of the loop shows how this problem leads to choice, then to effect, and keeps looping around back onto itself, thus generating a kind of engine that fuels the passive choice/decision-making process of the main character. When the problem or mystery gets solved, the loop is interrupted, and the situation is over.

Situations tend to evolve into episodic storytelling, which can be distracting and off-putting to audiences (and readers). Episodic writing is writing that is plagued by many narrative starts and stops, disconnected and standalone events, and mini-stories or situations within stories.

Sometimes, protagonists can appear to be the instigator of things, and so the events appear to be generated by them, but this is not the case. They do something stupid or make a blunder "out of the blue," and then an ensuing cascade of events forces them to react. The blunder or stupid mistake does not source from their moral component (i.e., their character), it is merely something they randomly do. Stories that portray the good and moral person caught up in the no-win scenario (*All Is Lost* (Lionsgate, 2013), *Gravity* (Warner Bros., 2013)) follows this passive loop structure.

These situations test the protagonist's stamina, will, or perseverance testing them to see if they have the metal to get through the crucible they've been thrust into by random chance, or being in the wrong place at the wrong time. Underdog stories follow this loop, unless they break out and make the story about why the protagonist is an underdog, examining the moral driver behind their passivity or underachievement (*Straw Dogs* (Cinema Releasing, 1971), *Falling Down* (Warner Bros., 1993)), and this —not merely surviving the situation—is the real lesson to be learned.

THE ACTIVE PROTAGONIST LOOP:

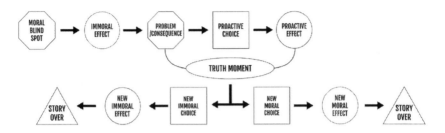

In stories with active protagonists, all action is generated from the main character's moral component. When the hero-heroine is driven by that core fear (moral blind spot), and then acts consistently with the fear (immoral effect), then all events in the story are directly or indirectly sourced from character, not generated as random external events.

Let's look at how this plays out with an example: Joe, the bank robber. Joe robs the bank because of his sense of entitlement, i.e., "the world owes me, so I get to take what I want" (*moral blind spot*), and he commits a crime (*immoral effect*); he does not blunder into a bank randomly and then pick up the wrong bag (filled with money) and accidentally robs the bank. Joe is the unwitting architect of his fall from grace. He is now a bank robber and on the run (*problem/consequence*), and must now figure out the best way to escape and not lose everything.

So, Joe calls up the best fixer he knows and arranges for his whole team to be snuck out of the country (*proactive choice*), leading to the entire gang becoming international criminals and targets for global law enforcement—something the gang did not sign up for! Joe's action creates a whole new complication, the gang becomes resentful and starts to conspire to perhaps turn Joe in, to save their skins (*proactive effect*). Joe continues around the loop making choices that lead to complications, that lead to effects that lead to new problems, and so on, until this loop is interrupted by Joes moment of personal change, i.e., the truth moment. Joe is the source of the loop's action. Joe drives events; events don't drive Joe.

ACTIVE PROTAGONIST LOOP BOTTOM RIGHT

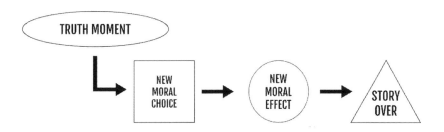

Through the course of choices, actions, and effects Joe realizes he isn't owed anything by the gang (*entitlement blind spot*)—he owes them. He owes them a chance to live normal lives and not go to jail because of him, so he does the right thing and sacrifices himself for the gang that has done so much for him (*truth moment*). This change then leads Joe down the right side of the bottom portion of the diagram: he turns himself in (*new moral choice*) and the gang escapes and their lives aren't ruined (new moral effect) and the story is over.

ACTIVE PROTAGONIST LOOP BOTTOM LEFT

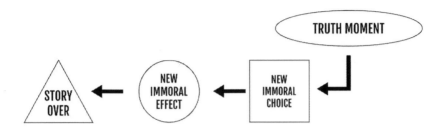

If however, Joe doesn't have a true moment of growth but decides that he must become even more self-centered in order to survive (ala Al Pacino in *The Godfather*), then he follows the left side of the bottom portion of the diagram: he sacrifices not himself, but the gang (*new immoral choice*), takes all the money, and then lives a life on the run, never sleeping in the same place more than one night, trusting no one (*new immoral effect*). The story ends with him alone in a cheap motel, surrounded by piles of money he can't spend, watching bad game shows in the dark and eating junk food—story over.

In the active protagonist loop, the protagonist has a blind spot in their moral outlook, a blind spot that leads them to generate a false belief about the world that in turn generates action that hurts other people (*immoral effect*). This hurtful action leads to a problem or consequence.

The *problem* or *consequence* is not some random, external thing forcing a reaction, no—quite the opposite—the problem only exists because of the moral component in action. This problem forces the protagonist the make a *proactive choice*/decision, leading to a *proactive effect* (they've created this mess, now they better do something about it). The loop portion of the diagram shows how this feeds back on itself, generating more choices and more effects that act as an engine to create and source scene-level conflict.

It is only when the protagonist has their moment of growth (truth moment), where they figure out what they are doing wrong morally and heal their base fear (moral blind spot), where they can then make a new moral choice and take further moral action, effectively ending the story. If they do not have a positive growth moment, then they disintegrate down the path of de-evolution, and their moral crisis deepens, perhaps to the point of self-destruction (again, think of the Al Pacino character in *The Godfather*).

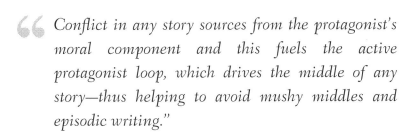 *Conflict in any story sources from the protagonist's moral component and this fuels the active protagonist loop, which drives the middle of any story—thus helping to avoid mushy middles and episodic writing."*

As stated at the beginning of this e-book, the moral premise is so important that it can stand alone as the keystone supporting all story development and story structure components, regardless of the story system, guru, or writing method you may prefer. Without a moral component you have a situation, a passive protagonist (even if they are shooting everything in sight), and you run the risk of episodic writing. With a moral component you have a story and a bulletproof engine for generating character-based drama and comedy readers will come back to time and time again.

GENERIC VS. PERSONAL
MORAL FLAW

One of the essential reasons for mastering the full complexity of the moral component of a story is that it helps the storyteller find a *personal* moral blind spot for the protagonist and not merely a generic flaw. A personal blind spot deepens the connection with the reader or audience and creates a more dramatic/comedic ending for any story. Falling back on generic and tropish moral problems is a trap that many writers fall into because they don't fully appreciate the importance of breaking down the "moral problem" into its basic components (blind spot, immoral effect, dynamic moral tension).

What do I mean by personal vs generic moral flaw? Let's walk through an example that we used earlier to illustrate the difference:

EXAMPLE: *The Verdict* (Twentieth Century Fox, 1982).

<u>Quick synopsis</u>: Frank, an ambulance-chasing, alcoholic, loser attorney uses people for personal gain and only sees people for what advantage they can get him. He uses people for financial leverage, and that is the only value he sees in people. Other human beings are targets, not people. Their worth is defined only by what Frank can get out of them for himself.

<u>What is his generic flaw?</u> Others story experts who have tackled this question have identified the following:

- Frank is *controlling and manipulative*, so he has to see this is wrong.
- Frank has to *learn how to act justly* in the world and not use people.
- Frank *selfish* and *self-centered* so he has to learn how to give selflessly.

These are all generic, not personal. They are generic because none of them describes *the why* they only describe *the what* of Frank's behavior. There is no clear light shown on his motivation for why he is controlling, or unjust, or selfish; just that he *is* one or more of those things.

This is what most writers do with their protagonists. The afflict them with a generic issue that appears to be personal but isn't. In the above scenario, we have no clue why Frank is acting the way he is acting; all we know is that he's doing it and that it's terrible and he needs to stop and be nicer.

This generic approach is not bad or wrong, but it robs the writer, and the reader/audience, of the fullest expression of the story. It is the "cheap seats" solution to deepening character at the expense of real depth. Consider the alternative, *personal*, approach.

What is his personal moral blind spot? The way you discover the personal flaw is by asking personal questions that get under the generic hood:

- Frank is acting like a jerk in the world. What would someone have to believe about themselves to justify such bad behavior?
- What is Frank afraid will happen if he does act justly, or is not controlling, or is not selfish?
- What horrible price will he have to pay if he doesn't act immorally?
- What is Frank terrified of exposing about himself, and so covers it up with his jerky behavior?

These are the kinds of questions (there are others) that must follow, once you the writer decides on the general conduct that will define your protagonist in their story world. You can't say "he's using others" and leave it at that. You have to ask, "why is he using others?" This is the only way to find out his real motivation for acting the way he does. Additionally, without knowing this motivation, you cannot have a convincing change for the protagonist at the end of the story. That final change/lesson-learned will end up as generic and lackluster as the original flaw, i.e., "he has to learn to be nice to people."

In this personal scenario, Frank is behaving badly in the world by using other people; they are targets, not people. Now ask the deeper, personal questions:

What is Frank afraid will happen if he doesn't take advantage of people?

He is afraid that if he doesn't "get his first," then he will be left out. It's a winner-take-all world, so get what you can get, while you can get it.

What price would he have to pay if he doesn't act immorally in the world?

He would be humiliated and rejected as worthless by the world, the price he would pay would be a life of shame.

What would he have to believe about the world to justify such behavior?

That people have no value or worth beyond what he can squeeze out of them.

What would he have to believe about himself to hold such a worldview?

That he has no value or worth, because he is human too, and all humans are worthless.

And so, this is Franks personal moral blind spot. He doesn't know he feels that way about himself, but that's what's motivating his behavior toward others. That's why it's his blind spot: he is blind to it, but others see it all the time played out in his behavior.

The whole story of *The Verdict* is about him fighting for the worth and value of a person that society has deemed worthless— a woman in a coma in a hospital bed. Frank learns, not that he has to be a champion and act justly, what he learns is that even a coma victim matters, and if someone like that matters, then he matters and has value, and he and she are both worth fighting for.

Do you see how this is more personal and not high-level or generic? Do you see how this has more heart and emotion, and how asking deeper character questions about real motivation gets you to the foundation of why a character is acting the way they do? Do you see how this makes for a better protagonist and story?

I cannot emphasize how powerful this technique of finding the personal moral blind spot can be for creating compelling and engaging protagonists. To help you fully master this technique, here are a few basic steps you can follow to begin to mature your personal approach to solving this problem in your stories.

HOW TO BUILD A PERSONAL MORAL FLAW

There are many strategies "out there" for writing a morally challenged protagonist, but I believe the vast majority of those strategies miss this critical piece we are discussing here, i.e., how to make the moral flaw personal and the foundation of motivation.

Almost everyone skims along the moral surface and avoids going deeper into the real character development that must be done.

So, while many writers start off in the right direction, but cut themselves off at the knees by not following through with the tough character questions that deepen their protagonist.

To transcend the generic, moral-flaw problem, make sure to do the following:

1. Make sure the moral issue of your protagonist is a moral issue and not superficial. This means understanding the meaning of "moral" in a storytelling context.

2. Ask the key personal questions that will uncover the real motivation for why your protagonist is acting the way he-she is acting. Always start with, "What would someone have to believe (incorrectly) about themselves to justify their bad behavior?"

- What is their worldview of others?
- What is their personal view of self?
- What is their greatest fear about what will happen if they change or get what they say they want?
- What price will they have to pay if they change?
- What fundamentally wrong core belief do they hold about who they are as a person?

3. Break down that motivation/belief into the three building blocks of the moral component: moral blind spot, immoral effect, and dynamic moral tension.

4. Make sure that whatever lesson is learned in the end, or whatever change your protagonist goes through, that it resolves the

original blind spot, or that it makes it worse (assuming the character doesn't change for the better, ala Michael Corleone in *The Godfather*).

If you implement these necessary steps with each new story and protagonist, your chances of having a deeper, more satisfying drama or comedy will be significantly increased, and readers or movie audiences will be more deeply engaged and committed to the protagonist's journey from start to finish. And, you will have avoided the biggest mistake most writers make when constructing a moral premise, i.e., falling into the generic moral flaw trap.

CONCLUSION

We've covered a lot of material in this small e-book. But, it is material that is barely covered at all in most other how-to creative writing books. At best, most gurus will offer a section of a chapter, or maybe a whole chapter devoted to the concept of the moral premise. But that's about all, and certainly not much, or any, direction teaching you how to create a convincing moral component. Most writers are on their own, blowing in the wind.

But, that is not you—at least it doesn't have to be. You now know more about how to develop proactive, morally flawed, and dramatically consistent characters than 99 per cent of most writers. You now have the tools and techniques available to you to not only validate whether or not you have a story before you start writing but to also develop that story into a compelling life-lesson about what it means to be human.

The moral basis of storytelling is the foundation of any real story. Most writers, through no fault of their own, are doomed to slog through the writing weeds and flounder in the story floodplains as they follow the consensus advice on how to write: "just do it." But once again, that is not you, at least it doesn't have to be. Now you know about development, moral components, blind spots, active protagonists, and stories vs situations.

The idea of "winging it" may still hold some seductive draw, but do not listen to the Siren's call, it will lure you to the rocks and your doom. Have confidence that, over time, all this information will trickle down from your conscious mind into your subconscious, and then into your creative process, and what was once mechanical process-procedures will become second nature and feel as natural to you as flight to an eagle.

As a conscious writer, you have a new path opening up before you, one that is crowded with solutions and options, and one that knows how to avoid the story woods and floodplain expertly. I'm very excited to have shared all this information with you because I fully expect you to take it all and move forward—and be brilliant.

THE END

CALL FOR REVIEWS

Buy Other Titles Here:

http://www.jefflyonsbooks.com

DID YOU LIKE THIS BOOK? THEN, I NEED YOU ...

Without reviews, indie books like this one are almost impossible to market.

If you purchased this book on any of the online book outlets, leaving a review will only take a minute and it will be incredibly helpful to me—and other readers.

The truth is, VERY few readers leave reviews. Please help me by being the exception.

Thank you in advance!

Jeff

ALSO BY JEFF LYONS

FICTION

Jack Be Dead: Revelation (bk #1)

13 Minutes

Terminus Station (coming)

The Abbess (coming)

NONFICTION

Anatomy of a Premise Line: How to Use Story and Premise Development for Writing Success

Rapid Story Development: How to Use the Enneagram-Story Connection to Become a Master Storyteller (coming)

Rapid Story Development: The Storyteller's Toolbox Volume One

RAPID STORY DEVELOPMENT E-BOOK SERIES

#1: Commercial Pace in Fiction and Creative Nonfiction

#2: Bust the Top Ten Creative Writing Myths to Become a Better Writer

#3: Ten Questions Every Writer Needs to Ask Before They Hire a Consultant

#4: Teams and Ensembles: How to Write Stories with Large Casts

#5: The Moral Premise–How to Build a Bulletproof Narrative Engine for Any Story

ABOUT THE AUTHOR

Jeff Lyons is a published author and story consultant with more than 25 years of experience in the publishing and entertainment industries. He has worked with literally thousands of screenwriters and novelists, including *New York Times* and *USA Today* bestselling authors. His writings on the craft of storytelling can be found in leading trade magazines like *Writer's Digest Magazine*, *Script Magazine*, and *The Writer Magazine*, among others. His book, *Anatomy of a Premise Line: How to Master Premise and Story Development for Writing Success* was published by Focal Press in 2015. Jeff is a popular presenter at leading writing industry trade conferences and has been invited to present and consult for the annual Producers Guild of America's "Power of Diversity Producers Fellowship Program," as well as for the Film Independent Screenwriting Lab. Jeff lives in Long Beach, California, has one weird cat, and desperately wants a dog. Visit www.jefflyonsbooks.com.

 facebook.com/storygeeks

twitter.com/storgeeks

instagram.com/jefflyonsbooks

[SEE NEXT PAGE]

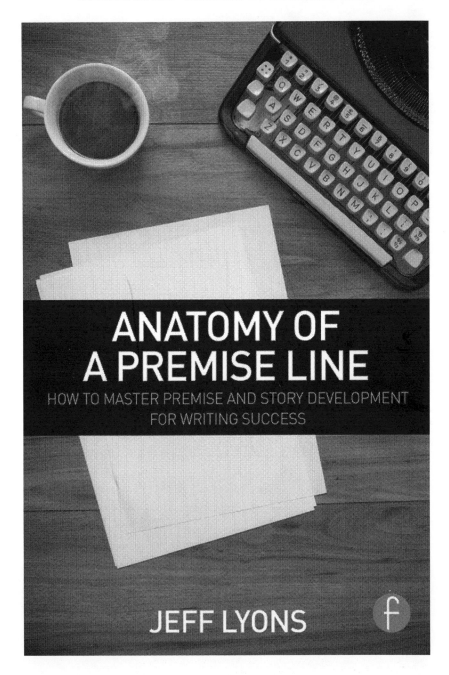

ANATOMY OF
A PREMISE LINE

HOW TO MASTER PREMISE AND STORY DEVELOPMENT
FOR WRITING SUCCESS

JEFF LYONS